Writing Strands

INTERMEDIATE 1

Focuses on skills such as organization,
description, and paragraphing

MASTERBOOKS® CURRICULUM

Author: Dave Marks

Master Books Creative Team:

Editors: Craig Froman
Shirley Rash
Becki Dudley

Design: Terry White

Cover Design: Diana Bogardus

Copy Editors:
Judy Lewis
Willow Meek

Curriculum Review:
Kristen Pratt
Laura Welch
Diana Bogardus

First printing: August 2017
Fourth printing: January 2020

ISBN: 978-1-68344-060-4
ISBN: 978-1-61458-621-0 (digital)

Unless otherwise noted, Scripture quotations are from the New King James Version of the Bible.

Printed in the United States of America

Please visit our website for other great titles:
www.masterbooks.com

About the Author

Since 1988, the *Writing Strands* series by **Dave Marks** has been helping homeschooling students develop their writing and communication skills. Dave was the founder of the National Writing Institute. He graduated from Western Michigan University, then received a master of arts degree from Central Michigan University. Dave retired after 30 years of teaching writing at all levels, from elementary school through the college level.

Table of Contents

Using *Writing Strands*

Features: The suggested weekly schedule enclosed has easy-to-manage lessons that guide the reading, worksheets, and all assessments. The pages of this guide are perforated and three-hole punched so materials are easy to tear out, hand out, grade, and store. Teachers are encouraged to adjust the schedule and materials needed in order to best work within their unique educational program.

The Four Strands: The series organizes writing into four strands: creative, argumentative, report and research, and expository writing. Success is contingent on how well students understand the following foundational skills taught in the lower levels: creative, basic, organizational, and descriptive writing. Students who have mastered these fundamental skills are ready to apply them to the abstract subject matter of the upper-level books in the series.

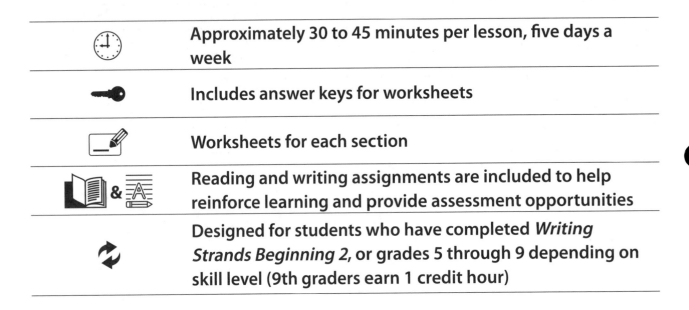

	Approximately 30 to 45 minutes per lesson, five days a week
	Includes answer keys for worksheets
	Worksheets for each section
	Reading and writing assignments are included to help reinforce learning and provide assessment opportunities
	Designed for students who have completed *Writing Strands Beginning 2*, or grades 5 through 9 depending on skill level (9th graders earn 1 credit hour)

Course Objectives: Students completing this course will

- ✔ Understand that ideas in sentences are connected, and that ideas flow from one sentence to the next.
- ✔ Learn to identify and analyze the elements of plot in literature.
- ✔ List the main points in the summary of a story.
- ✔ Understand that there is a voice which speaks to the reader.

- ✔ Realize the structure of description, and start descriptions with general statements.
- ✔ Use past tense, present tense, and future tense.
- ✔ Recognize a character's physical positions and realize how position controls what characters know.

Course Description

Introduction: *Writing Strands Intermediate 1* is designed to give students a grounding in the process of giving others their thoughts in written form. This level is designed for any student who has completed the exercises in *Writing Strands Beginner 2*. This level is designed for 4th to 9th grade students, depending on skill level. Of course, 5th and 9th grade students would write differently but both can benefit in learning the skills presented in this level. Generally, we recommend using this level in Grade 5 but the skill level of the student should always guide placement.

Lessons are easy to teach and do not require preparation. Sit with the student, read the lesson together, and discuss anything that is not clear. Remember, composition is a skill that is learned over time. We recommend you purchase the *Writing Strands Teaching Companion*. This invaluable resource will save you a great deal of time, and it will help your students learn more quickly.

Much of the planning and detail of the writing process is presented here. The writing exercises in this level are in four categories: basic, creation, organization, and description. The exercises in each of these areas will guide the student in the development of necessary skills for writing.

The books in this series are designed for one school year each, which should include our reading program. We recommend that you alternate each writing exercise with a week of reading and discussing books and ideas. In this way, you will have a full school year of language arts. We have made it easy by providing a Daily Schedule to follow.

The reading half of any language arts program should involve reading and talking about books and ideas. The reading section found in the *Writing Strands Teaching Companion* provides extra guidance to get the most out of the reading week.

Grading Options for This Course: It is always the prerogative of an educator to assess student grades however he or she might deem best. For *Writing Strands*, the teacher is to evaluate primarily whether a student has mastered a particular skill or whether the student needs additional experience. A teacher may rank these on a five-point scale as follows:

Skill Mastered				**Needs Experience**
5 (equals an A)	4(B)	3(C)	2(D)	1 (equals an F)

A — Student showed complete mastery of concepts with no errors.

B — Student showed mastery of concepts with minimal errors.

C — Student showed partial mastery of concepts. Review of some concepts is needed.

D — Student showed minimal understanding of concepts. Review is needed.

F — Student did not show understanding of concepts. Review is needed.

Note: See Weekly Skills Writing Mastery Chart on pages 13–14 for basic assessment of the Writing Skills in the course.

How to Make *Writing Strands* Work for You

1. Students should keep a writing folder or 3-ring binder to contain all written work, which can be kept for the next level. This will give the teacher a place to store and record the student's progress and skills.

2. The teacher and student should track what the students have learned and what they still need to learn. Here are some ways to do that:

   a) After every assignment, the teacher or student should fill in the Progress Report that follows the assignment.

   b) The teacher should fill out the Weekly Skills Writing Mastery Chart as the student completes assignments.

   c) Writers can always learn new things. Young writers should not expect to fix all their problems right away. The teacher can keep track of the problems they have noted but the student has not yet solved using the Spelling List and List of Problems to Solve.

3. Many of the exercises suggest that the teacher will work with the student during the writing period, reading what the students have written. If this is done, it will serve two purposes:

   a) It will give the student constant feedback and will allow the teacher to catch many writing problems before they appear in the final papers.

   b) It will greatly cut down on the teacher's correcting time. Most of the proofreading can be done during writing time, so even though students will be writing much more than they previously have, the teacher should be able to help the students more using less time.

4. We recommend teachers use the *Writing Strands Teaching Companion* to help with the writing process. It can help a great deal with the development of writing skills, including grammar, spelling, and other challenging areas.

5. Prior to beginning this course, it is suggested that teacher and student read through the Helpful Terms found in the back of the book.

Principles of *Writing Strands*

1. John 1:1 says, "the Word was made flesh and dwelled among us." God used the Living Word, Jesus Christ, to reveal Himself to us, and so as His followers, the ability to communicate clearly with words is intrinsically important to how we express Christ to the world.

2. Every person needs to learn to express ideas and feelings in writing.

3. There is no one right way to write anything.

4. The ability to write is not an expression of a body of knowledge that can be learned like a list of vocabulary words.

5. Writing teachers and their students both learn in any effective writing situation.

6. The product of each student's writing efforts must be seen as a success for the following reasons:

    a) A student in a writing experience is not in competition with anyone else.

    b) There is no perfect model against which any effort can be compared for evaluation, so there is no best way for any student to write.

    c) Every controlled writing experience will help students improve the ability to express themselves.

7. All student writing efforts are worthy of praise. The most help any writing teacher can give at any point is to show, in a positive way, what is good about a piece and how it might be improved.

8. Any writing lesson assigned that does not receive a teacher's reinforcement and suggestions represents a missed opportunity for the student.

9. All writing at any level is hard work, and every writer should be encouraged to feel the pride of authorship. Students should learn that writing is fun, exciting, and rewarding.

10. All young authors need to be published. This can be accomplished by having their work read to other family members, posted on bulletin boards, hung on the refrigerator, printed in "books," or read by other family members.

Writing Guidelines

Why should we follow guidelines, or rules, when we write? Guidelines help us communicate better. They provide us with the things that we should do, that we agree to do, and that make life nicer for everyone if we do them.

An example of a writing rule is the rule that says every sentence must start with a capital letter. This is written down, and we all must write using this rule. It helps us know when a new sentence is beginning. Following this rule helps us to communicate better.

Our list of guidelines consists of just a few rules to keep in mind when you write. We suggest students review the rules before each writing exercise:

1. Use exclamation points sparingly. Overuse makes any writing look amateurish and fuzzy. If you are saying something that is important, the way you say it should be strong enough so that you do not have to tell your reader that it is important by using exclamation points at the end of your sentences.

2. Do not underline the titles of your papers. The only time there should be an underline in one of your titles is when you use the names of books or magazines.

3. Skip a line after the title in any paper you are giving to someone else to read.

4. Never write "The End" at the end of anything you write for a school exercise.

5. Do not try writing humor until you have studied it and really know the difference between being funny and being corny.

6. Do not skip a line between paragraphs.

7. Always leave a margin at the bottom of each page.

8. Check your papers for clichés before you write the final drafts. Please see the Helpful Terms section in the back of this book for more information on clichés.

Reading and Evaluating Literature

One of the goals at Master Books is to help students develop critical thinking skills. You will notice throughout these lessons that students are encouraged to answer the same questions about each piece of literature they read. This is intentional and designed to help them think about what they read. We want these questions to become second nature as they progress through life and encounter literature from various sources. It is okay if your student cannot answer all of the questions each week, but you should see a progression in their ability to analyze what they are reading.

Studying the Literature of the Bible: Each week students will read biblical passages as assigned, as well as a book his or her teacher will assign. During the course of this year, students will be focusing on the plot of a story during the literature lessons, applying this to the biblical passages.

The Bible is a collection of 66 God-inspired books of history, poetry, wisdom, prophecy, letters, and revelation, written by over 40 different authors ranging from shepherds to kings, over the time span of 1,500 years, all revealing God's Word and showing us the way of salvation through Jesus Christ. Knowing that the word of God is "living and active" and able to "discern the thoughts and intentions of the heart," it is always a good idea to pray for the Lord's wisdom and understanding before each biblical reading assignment. The Genres of Biblical Literature guide will help your student understand and identify the various genres in Scripture, and the following guideline should help you gain the most from every biblical passage.

Step One: Read each passage, keeping in mind the characters and the cultural and historical setting of the text. (This can often be found in the introductory material to a book in the Bible.)

Step Two: Determine the genre of the literature (history, poetry, prophecy, proverbs, letters, parables, etc.).

Step Three: Look for the intended meaning. One way to do this is to ask questions like "What fallen or sinful condition is being highlighted in this passage?" or "What prompted the author to write this passage?" (Is this message about sin, salvation, faith, hope, etc.?)

Step Four: Seek other passages to help define the meaning (Scripture interprets Scripture).

Step Five: Once the original meaning is understood, seed to find a simple life application.

Reading and Evaluating Literature

Studying Classical or Contemporary Literature: The book chosen can be short enough to be read within an hour, or longer to be read over the course of the full week. In addition to reading various biblical passages, every other week students will be reading and discussing a book selected by his or her teacher. When reading classical or contemporary books, a primary concern should always be the worldview or moral viewpoint of the author. A writer who believes that God created the heavens and the earth and who created people in His own image realizes that God instilled us with purpose and meaning. This writing will be distinctly different from an atheistic author who most likely believes that the earth and everything in the universe came about by random chance events, and that life rose from non-life with no direction, intention, or purpose. So, in your evaluation of fiction, keep in mind these five principles, provided for you with each book passage portion you choose to read during this course:

Step One: Determine the genre of the literature (historical fiction, fantasy, drama, Western, mystery, science fiction, poetry, biography, etc.).

Step Two: Read the book, keeping in mind the main setting of the text and the primary roles of each character.

Step Three: Look for the flow of the story.

Step Four: What is the book's message or what do you think it is trying to teach you?

Step Five: Does this message agree with what the Bible teaches? Why or why not?

Genres of Written Literature

Poetry: Stylistic writing that utilizes devices such as meter, rhythm, metaphor, and/or rhyme (among many others); to express feelings and ideas or to tell a story. Poetry has several subgenres, including but not limited to: **Narrative, Lyric, Epic, Dramatic, and Satire**.

Prose: Writing that follows a straightforward grammatical structure of complete sentences and paragraphs. It resembles everyday speech. Both fiction and nonfiction are subgenres.

Fiction: Writing that is based on imaginary characters and events. There are many subgenres of fiction including but not limited to:

Fantasy	Mystery
Western	Detective Story
Romance	Dystopia
Science Fiction	Historical Fiction
Thriller	

Nonfiction: Writing based upon the lives, events, and/or ideas of real people. Subgenres include but are not limited to:

Autobiography	Diaries and Journals
Biography	Textbooks
Commentary	Travel
Theology	Self-help
Legal	Newspapers
True Crime	

Genres of Biblical Literature

The Bible contains numerous types of literature, or "genres," each with its own writing style. While some books of the Bible could fit into more than one genre, the following chart categorizes them by their primary genre only. Understanding the genre helps us identify the main purpose and setting of the book. Even though these books were written a long time ago, it is important to remember that they can and should help us grow spiritually today. (2 Tim 3:16-17)

Law: The first five books in the Bible that describe the foundation of the world and the beginnings of history. They contain God's promise to Abraham to make of his descendants a great nation by whom all the families of the earth will be blessed, as well as the laws given by God (through Moses) to the people of Israel.

Historical Narrative: Books in the Bible that describe historical events that happened in the Old and New Testaments. They primarily cover the history of the Jewish nation (Old Testament) and the history of the early Christian church (New Testament).

Poetry: Books that deal with important questions and issues of life, such as suffering, daily living, relationships, and the nature of God. Often written in a poetic style.

Prophecy: These books record God's messages to the people in the Old Testament as spoken through the individual prophets. In the Bible, a "prophet" was a person called to speak for God. They spoke the words God gave them. Sometimes the prophets predicted future events, and sometimes they addressed current issues and events.

Gospels: These are the eyewitness accounts of the life, death, and resurrection of Jesus.

Letters: Letters written to individual people or groups of people, each with a specific message or purpose. These letters have a style similar to letters we would write today, including a greeting, a body, and a closing.

CONTINUED ON NEXT PAGE➜

Genres of Biblical Literature

OLD TESTAMENT

Law	Historical Narrative
Genesis	Joshua
Exodus	1 Samuel
Leviticus	2 Samuel
Numbers	Ezra
Deuteronomy	Judges
	1 Kings

Poetry	
Job	2 Kings
Ecclesiastes	Nehemiah
Psalms	Ruth
Song of Solomon	1 Chronicles
Proverbs	2 Chronicles
	Esther

Prophecy

Major Prophets	Minor Prophets	
Isaiah	Hosea	Nahum
Jeremiah	Joel	Habakkuk
Lamentations	Amos	Zephaniah
Ezekiel	Obadiah	Haggai
Daniel	Jonah	Zechariah
	Micah	Malachi

NEW TESTAMENT

Gospels	Historical Narrative
Matthew	Acts
Mark	
Luke	
John	

Letters	
Romans	Titus
1 Corinthians	Philemon
2 Corinthians	Hebrews
Galatians	James
Ephesians	1 Peter
Philippians	2 Peter
Colossians	1 John
1 Thessalonians	2 John
2 Thessalonians	3 John
1 Timothy	Jude
2 Timothy	Revelation

Weekly Skills Writing Mastery Chart

Student Name: _____

Teacher: As your student completes an assignment, indicate whether each objective has been met. If your student needs experience with an objective, revisit this assignment or this skill before proceeding to the next *Writing Strands* level.

Lesson 1: How a Sentence Does It Skill Area: Basic	Skill Met	Revisit
1. Decide what information you want to give to your reader.		
2. Organize this information for your reader.		
3. Write a sentence containing the information in that order		
4. Learn about compound and complex sentences.		
Lesson 2: Connections Skill Area: Organization		
1. Understand that ideas in sentences can be connected.		
2. Understand that ideas can flow from one sentence to the next.		
3. Make ideas in your writing flow from one point to another.		
Lesson 3: The Main Points Skill Area: Organization		
1. Recognize the main points in a story.		
2. List the main points in your summary of a story.		
Lesson 4: I Feel Skill Area: Description		
1. Decide how you felt about something that happened to you.		
2. Understand that it is possible to explain how you felt about an event.		
3. Describe how you felt about an event.		
4. Practice writing compound sentences.		

Lesson 5: My Mistake Skill Area: Organization	Skill Met	Revisit
1. Admit that you did something that was a mistake.		
2. Analyze what you did.		
3. Recognize the action that caused the mistake.		
Lesson 6: Narrative Voice Skill Area: Creative		
1. Understand that writers create voices which speak to their readers.		
2. Understand that all the voices writers use do not work in the same way.		
3. Understand that writers must choose a voice to talk to their reader.		
Lesson 7: Controlling Point of View Skill Area: Basic		
1. Understand the different narrative voices.		
2. Control the use of person in your writing.		
Lesson 8: Changing Tenses Skill Area: Basic		
1. Understand how past tense works.		
2. Understand how a change from past to present tense in a story changes the story.		
3. Change past tense to present tense in a story.		
Lesson 9: Past, Present, and Future Skill Area: Basic		
1. Learn and practice the use of past, present, and future tenses.		

	Skill Met	Revisit
Lesson 10: Paragraphs **Skill Area: Basic**		
1. Organize a group of ideas.		
2. Write a sentence that introduces a group of ideas.		
3. Construct a paragraph based on a group of ideas.		
Lesson 11: My Home, Part 1 **Skill Area: Description**		
1. Understand the layout of a building.		
2. Show relationships of spaces in floor plans.		
3. Use a bird's-eye view.		
4. Create a drawing from what you see.		
Lesson 12: My Home, Part 2 **Skill Area: Description**		
1. Understand the structure of description.		
2. Describe a building starting with general statements.		
3. Support general statements with detail.		
4. Turn graphic representations into verbal descriptions (drawings into words) so that someone else can make a floor plan from it.		
5. Study your own work and decide if it needs to be changed or made better.		
6. Add to or change your writing to make it better.		
Lesson 13: Describing a Thought Problem **Skill Area: Organization**		
1. Picture a situation in your mind which would be a problem.		
2. Describe what such an imaginary situation would be like.		
3. Solve a thought problem.		

	Skill Met	Revisit
Lesson 14: Things Change **Skill Area: Description**		
1. Learn that things do change.		
2. Understand that descriptions of changes can be organized.		
3. Describe changes so they are easy to understand.		
4. Write a paper that has an introduction and a conclusion.		
Lesson 15: From Where I Was **Skill Area: Description**		
1. Understand that characters in fiction must be in specific places.		
2. Understand that position (place) determines what characters can experience.		
3. Understand that you can control the position of your first person narrative voice characters.		
Lesson 16: Attitude in Description, Part 1 **Skill Area: Creative**		
1. Understand that authors give attitudes to their narrative voices.		
2. Understand that authors give attitudes to their narrative voices.		
Lesson 17: Attitude in Description, Part 2 **Skill Area: Description**		
1. Understand that authors give attitudes to their narrative voices.		
2. Understand that you can give your reader feelings by the attitudes you give your first-person characters.		
Lesson 18: The Long and Short of It **Skill Area: Creative**		
1. Understand that sentence length is important.		
2. Control the length of your sentences to help your reader appreciate and understand what you have to say.		

Spelling List

The research on how people learn to spell indicates that spelling mastery comes from spelling words correctly through the practice of writing. Words studied in isolation, in abstracted lists, do not carry over from the study to correct use.

This page is not to be used as a word list to be memorized. Rather, it is for the instructor and the teacher to keep a record of the words the student has problems spelling. Turn back to this page after each exercise, and record the words that the student wants to work on in the future weeks.

If the student picks out one word a week — one that is used constantly — and the next week is spent working on that one problem word, the student will remember it much better than if it had been memorized for a spelling test. More importantly, in two or three years, the student will have mastered several words without the frustration of unsuccessful testing.

To help the student learn how to spell the problem word, help the student find the word's origins in a large dictionary, study the prefixes and suffixes, and practice the basic spelling rules that apply.

The teacher might check the *Teaching Companion* for more on this subject.

_____

_____

_____

_____

_____

_____

_____

_____

_____

_____

_____

_____

_____

_____

_____

_____

_____

_____

List of Problems to Solve

Teacher: As the teacher and student work through this book, use this page as a convenient place to keep a running list of the problems that should be solved throughout the year. Keep in mind that the student will have years to work on writing skills. Progress is the goal rather than perfection.

Record here the writing problems the student has not yet solved. For each exercise, point out only one way to improve the mechanics of the writing. This allows students to master the concept without feeling overwhelmed. Check our *Writing Strands Teaching Companion* for more on this process and why it is so very important.

_____

_____

_____

_____

_____

_____

_____

_____

_____

_____

_____

First Semester Suggested Daily Schedule

Date	Day	Assignment	Due Date	✓	Grade
		First Semester-First Quarter			
Week 1	Day 1	Read introductory portion • Pages 6–15 Writing Lesson 1: How a Sentence Does It • Pages 23–24			
	Day 2	Organizing information • Page 25			
	Day 3	Constructing sentence • Pages 26–27			
	Day 4	Rewriting sentence • Pages 28–29			
	Day 5	Write paper • Pages 30–32 • Student Progress Report • Page 33			
Week 2	Day 6	Reading Lesson 1: Plot in Literature • Page 34			
	Day 7	Discuss assigned passage • Page 35			
	Day 8	Read and discuss with teacher • Page 36			
	Day 9	Complete activity • Page 37			
	Day 10	Read and discuss assigned book • Page 38			
Week 3	Day 11	Writing Lesson 2: Connections • Pages 39–40			
	Day 12	Making information flow • Page 41			
	Day 13	Creating sentences that flow • Page 42			
	Day 14	Write list for paragraph • Page 43			
	Day 15	Writing paragraph from ideas list • Page 44 Student Progress Report • Page 45			
Week 4	Day 16	Reading Lesson 2: Story Plot and Sequence of Events • Page 46			
	Day 17	Discuss assigned passage • Page 47			
	Day 18	Read and discuss with teacher • Page 48			
	Day 19	Complete activity • Page 49			
	Day 20	Read and discuss assigned book • Page 50			
Week 5	Day 21	Writing Lesson 3: The Main Points • Pages 51–52			
	Day 22	Read a story • Page 53			
	Day 23	Using an organization outline • Page 54			
	Day 24	Write a paper on story • Page 55			
	Day 25	Continue to write paper • Pages 56–57 • Student Progress Report Page 58			
Week 6	Day 26	Reading Lesson 3: Cause and Effect in Plot • Page 59			
	Day 27	Discuss assigned passage • Page 60			
	Day 28	Read and discuss with teacher • Page 61			
	Day 29	Complete activity • Page 62			
	Day 30	Read and discuss assigned book • Pages 63–64			
Week 7	Day 31	Writing Lesson 4: I Feel • Pages 65–66			
	Day 32	Writing list of experiences • Page 67			
	Day 33	Writing description of feelings • Page 68			
	Day 34	Write topic sentence • Page 69			
	Day 35	Description Worksheet • Pages 70–71 Student Progress Report • Page 72			

Date	Day	Assignment	Due Date	✓	Grade
Week 8	Day 36	Reading Lesson 4: Character and Plot • Page 73			
	Day 37	Discuss assigned passage • Page 74			
	Day 38	Read and discuss with teacher • Page 75			
	Day 39	Complete activity • Page 76			
	Day 40	Read and discuss assigned book • Pages 77–78			
Week 9	Day 41	Writing Lesson 5: My Mistake • Page 79			
	Day 42	Analyzing mistakes • Page 80			
	Day 43	List of actions into sentences • Page 81			
	Day 44	Rewriting sentences • Page 82			
	Day 45	Write your paper • Pages 83–84 Student Progress Report • Page 85			
First Semester–Second Quarter					
Week 1	Day 46	Reading Lesson 5: Driving Forces in Plot • Page 86			
	Day 47	Discuss assigned passage • Page 87			
	Day 48	Read and discuss with teacher • Page 88			
	Day 49	Complete activity • Page 89			
	Day 50	Read and discuss assigned book • Page 90			
Week 2	Day 51	Writing Lesson 6: Narrative Voice • Pages 91–92			
	Day 52	Finish short story • Page 93			
	Day 53	Rewrite short story • Page 94			
	Day 54	Finish another short story • Pages 95–96			
	Day 55	Define terms • Page 97 • Student Progress Report • Page 98			
Week 3	Day 56	Reading Lesson 6: Elements of Plot: Exposition • Page 99			
	Day 57	Discuss assigned passage • Page 100			
	Day 58	Read and discuss with teacher • Page 101			
	Day 59	Complete activity • Page 102			
	Day 60	Read and discuss assigned book • Pages 103–104			
Week 4	Day 61	Writing Lesson 7: Controlling Point of View • Page 105			
	Day 62	Writing in third person • Pages 106–107			
	Day 63	Writing in second person • Page 108			
	Day 64	Writing in first person • Page 109			
	Day 65	Explain the three narrative voices • Page 110 Student Progress Report • Page 111			
Week 5	Day 66	Reading Lesson 7: Elements of Plot: Complication Pages 112–113			
	Day 67	Discuss assigned passage • Page 114			
	Day 68	Read and discuss with teacher • Page 115			
	Day 69	Complete activity • Page 116			
	Day 70	Read and discuss assigned book • Pages 117–118			

Date	Day	Assignment	Due Date	✓	Grade
Week 6	Day 71	Writing Lesson 8: Changing Tenses • Page 119			
	Day 72	Creating a story • Page 120			
	Day 73	Writing out sentences • Pages 121–122			
	Day 74	Completing the story • Page 123			
	Day 75	Read what you have written to someone else • Page 124 Student Progress Report • Page 125			
Week 7	Day 76	Reading Lesson 8: Elements of Plot: Rising Action • Page 126–127			
	Day 77	Discuss assigned passage • Page 128			
	Day 78	Read and discuss with teacher • Page 129			
	Day 79	Complete activity • Page 130			
	Day 80	Read and discuss assigned book • Pages 131–132			
Week 8	Day 81	Writing Lesson 9: Past, Present, and Future • Page 133			
	Day 82	Making characters think • Page 134			
	Day 83	Start your story • Pages 135–136			
	Day 84	Continue your story • Page 137			
	Day 85	Finish your story • Page 138 • Student Progress Report • Page 139			
Week 9	Day 86	Reading Lesson 9: Elements of Plot: Climax • Page 140			
	Day 87	Discuss assigned passage • Page 141			
	Day 88	Read and discuss with teacher • Page 142			
	Day 89	Complete activity • Page 143			
	Day 90	Read and discuss assigned book • Page 144 Problems I Have Solved This First Semester • Page 145			
		Mid-Term Grade			

Second Semester Suggested Daily Schedule

Date	Day	Assignment	Due Date	✓	Grade
		Second Semester-Third Quarter			
Week 1	Day 91	Writing Lesson 10: Paragraphs • Pages 147–148			
	Day 92	Organizing items • Pages 149–150			
	Day 93	Write a topic sentence • Page 151			
	Day 94	Writing an organized paragraph • Pages 152–153			
	Day 95	Write your paragraph • Pages 154–155 Student Progress Report • Page 156			
Week 2	Day 96	Reading Lesson 10: Elements of Plot: Falling Action Page 157			
	Day 97	Discuss assigned passage • Page 158			
	Day 98	Read and discuss with teacher • Page 159			
	Day 99	Complete activity • Page 160			
	Day 100	Read and discuss assigned book • Pages 161–162			
Week 3	Day 101	Writing Lesson 11: My Home, Part 1 • Pages 163–165			
	Day 102	Rough drawing • Page 166			
	Day 103	Floor plans • Page 167			
	Day 104	Floor plans continued • Page 168			
	Day 105	Finish floor plan • Page 169 Student Progress Report • Page 170			
Week 4	Day 106	Reading Lesson 11: Elements of Plot: Resolution • Page 171			
	Day 107	Discuss assigned passage • Page 172			
	Day 108	Read and discuss with teacher • Page 173			
	Day 109	Complete activity • Page 174			
	Day 110	Read and discuss assigned book • Pages 175–176			
Week 5	Day 111	Writing Lesson 12: My Home, Part 2 • Pages 177–178			
	Day 112	Writing first and second paragraphs • Pages 179–180			
	Day 113	Writing third paragraph and conclusion • Pages 181–182			
	Day 114	Write paper on floor plan • Pages 183–185			
	Day 115	Getting paper back • Page 186 Student Progress Report • Page 187			
Week 6	Day 116	Reading Lesson 12: Elements of Plot: Putting It All Together Page 188			
	Day 117	Discuss assigned passage • Page 189			
	Day 118	Read and discuss with teacher • Page 190			
	Day 119	Complete activity • Page 191			
	Day 120	Read and discuss assigned book • Page 192			

Date	Day	Assignment	Due Date	✓	Grade
Week 7	Day 121	Writing Lesson 13: Describing a Thought Problem Pages 193–194			
	Day 122	Describe and solve a thought problem • Pages 195–196			
	Day 123	Making outline of ideas • Pages 197–198			
	Day 124	Finish paper • Page 199			
	Day 125	Read your paper to someone else • Page 200 Student Progress Report • Page 201			
Week 8	Day 126	Reading Lesson 13: Plot: Conflict with Individuals • Page 202			
	Day 127	Discuss assigned passage • Page 203			
	Day 128	Read and discuss with teacher • Page 204			
	Day 129	Complete activity • Page 205			
	Day 130	Read and discuss assigned book • Page 206			
Week 9	Day 131	Writing Lesson 14: Things Change • Pages 207–208			
	Day 132	Writing descriptions • Pages 209–210			
	Day 133	How things look and feel • Pages 211–212			
	Day 134	Writing conclusion • Page 213			
	Day 135	Write paper • Pages 214–215 Student Progress Report • Page 216			
		Second Semester-Fourth Quarter			
Week 1	Day 136	Reading Lesson 14: Plot: Conflict with Society • Page 217			
	Day 137	Discuss assigned passage • Page 218			
	Day 138	Read and discuss with teacher • Page 219			
	Day 139	Complete activity • Page 220			
	Day 140	Read and discuss assigned book • Pages 221–222			
Week 2	Day 141	Writing Lesson 15: From Where I Was • Pages 223–224			
	Day 142	Character positions • Page 225			
	Day 143	Write your scenario • Page 226			
	Day 144	Writing first account • Page 227			
	Day 145	Writing second account • Page 228 Student Progress Report • Page 229			
Week 3	Day 146	Reading Lesson 15: Plot: Conflict with Setting • Page 230			
	Day 147	Discuss assigned passage • Page 231			
	Day 148	Read and discuss with teacher • Page 232			
	Day 149	Complete activity • Page 233			
	Day 150	Read and discuss assigned book • Page 234			
Week 4	Day 151	Writing Lesson 16: Attitude In Description, Part 1 Pages 235–236			
	Day 152	Writing about what one sees • Page 237			
	Day 153	Writing about what one hears • Page 238			
	Day 154	Writing about what one smells • Page 239			
	Day 155	Putting it all together • Page 240 Student Progress Report • Page 241			

Date	Day	Assignment	Due Date	✓	Grade
Week 5	Day 156	Reading Lesson 16: Plot: Internal Conflict • Page 242			
	Day 157	Discuss assigned passage • Page 243			
	Day 158	Read and discuss with teacher • Page 244			
	Day 159	Complete activity • Page 245			
	Day 160	Read and discuss assigned book • Page 246			
Week 6	Day 161	Writing Lesson 17: Attitude In Description, Part 2 • Page 247			
	Day 162	Writing about what one hears • Page 248			
	Day 163	Writing about what one smells • Page 249			
	Day 164	Putting it all together • Page 250			
	Day 165	Write final copy of both pieces • Page 251 Student Progress Report • Page 252			
Week 7	Day 166	Reading Lesson 17: Reviewing the Importance of Plot, Part 1 Page 253			
	Day 167	Discuss assigned passage • Page 254			
	Day 168	Read and discuss with teacher • Page 255			
	Day 169	Complete activity • Page 256			
	Day 170	Read and discuss assigned book • Pages 257–258			
Week 8	Day 171	Writing Lesson 18: The Long and Short of It • Page 259			
	Day 172	Write about an event • Page 260			
	Day 173	Finish writing about an event • Page 261			
	Day 174	Write final copy • Pages 262–263			
	Day 175	Read your paper to someone else • Page 264 Student Progress Report • Page 265			
Week 9	Day 176	Reading Lesson 18: Reviewing the Importance of Plot, Part 2 Page 266			
	Day 177	Discuss assigned passage • Page 267			
	Day 178	Read and discuss with teacher • Page 268			
	Day 179	Complete activity • Page 269			
	Day 180	Read and discuss assigned book • Page 270 Problems I Have Solved This Second Semester • Page 271			
		Final Grade			

Writing

I will work through the process of sentence writing to show you how easy it is, and then you will do the same thing. When you are done you will be able to say, "Writing really good sentences is easy."

There are only 3 steps:

1. Pick a subject and list what information you want to give to your reader.

_____

2. Organize this information in the best way for your reader to understand it.

_____

3. Write a sentence containing that information in that order.

_____

Step 1: Pick subject of sentence and list pieces of information

The first thing I have to do is to pick the subject. I have to decide what I want my reader to know. This could be anything. I will show you how easy this first step is by listing some possibilities.

I might want to tell my reader about:

1. "Dog," my dog (Dog really is her name)

2. Where I live

3. What I like to eat best

4. Which coat is best for me

5. How graceful Great Blue Herons are

6. My fall

As you can see, it does not make any difference what I want to talk about. You will see that the process is the same for all subjects. And this process is SIMPLE.

I will pick 6. My fall. Now that I have the subject of my sentence, I have to decide what I want my reader to know about that subject. In this case, I have to decide what parts of my falling I want my reader to understand.

Objectives:

❶ Decide what information you want to give to your reader.

❷ Organize this information for your reader.

❸ Write a sentence containing the information in that order.

❹ Learn about compound and complex sentences.

CONTINUED ON NEXT PAGE➜

This is what happened:

> After we had finished eating Thanksgiving dinner at my aunt's house, I said I would help clear the table. The women there said that I should not, that they would do it. I said, "I am really very good at this, and I have had lots of practice." I put all the plates I could reach into one pile in front of me. When I picked up this pile, I caught the edge of the tablecloth with my hand and pulled it behind me when I turned toward the kitchen. Of course, all the other dishes came with it. The weight of pulling all the things off the table made me lose my balance, and I started to fall. To save myself, I threw the pile of dishes I was carrying forward, but that did not help, and I fell into the center of a great pile of food and broken dishes. I was so embarrassed I could have hidden for a month.

That is the information I want to give my reader. It is too much detail for one sentence, so I will not be able to give it all at the same time. What I have to do is list the pieces of information I can give in one sentence, like this:

(A) Thanksgiving dinner

(B) Helped clear the table

(C) Pulled off the tablecloth

(D) Dropped dishes

(E) Fell into mess

(F) I was embarrassed

Step 2: Organize information

Step 2 says that I have to organize the information to make it easy to understand. In this paragraph, I will put letters before the information in the same order as the things happened in the event so I can see what to put first and second and so on.

> After we had finished eating (A) Thanksgiving dinner at my aunt's house, I said I would (B) help clear the table. All the women there said that I should not, that they would do it. I said, "I am really very good at this, and I have had lots of practice." I put all the plates I could reach into one pile in front of me. When I picked up this pile, (C) I caught the edge of the tablecloth with my hand and pulled it behind me when I turned toward the kitchen. Of course all the other dishes came with it. The weight of pulling all the things on the table made me lose my balance, and I started to fall. To save myself, (D) I threw the pile of dishes I was carrying forward, but that did not help, and (E) I fell into the center of a great pile of food and broken dishes. (F) I was so embarrassed I could have hidden for a month.

I have listed these pieces of information again to make it easier to organize them.

(A) Thanksgiving dinner

(B) Helped clear the table

(C) Pulled off the tablecloth

(D) Dropped dishes

(E) Fell into mess

(F) I was embarrassed

The first thing I will want my reader to know is that I was really embarrassed. So, I will start my sentence with (F).

1. (F) I was really embarrassed

Since I should tell my readers when I was embarrassed, I will use (A) next.

2. (A) Thanksgiving dinner

The rest of the information can be in the order in which it happened: (B), (C), (D), and (E). This will now give my reader the information about my fall in this order:

1. I was embarrassed

2. Thanksgiving dinner

3. Helped clear the table

4. Pulled off the tablecloth

5. Dropped dishes

6. Fell into mess

Step 3: Write the sentence

All I have to do now is construct a sentence with this information in this order. To show you what the reordering did to the sentence, I will put letters in front of the pieces of information in my new sentence so that it will be easy for you to spot where they came from in the original list of what happened.

> I was really (F) embarrassed at (A) Thanksgiving dinner when (B) I helped clear the table because (C) I caught the edge of the tablecloth, pulling it and all the other dishes with it, and, (D) dropping the dishes I was carrying, (E) fell into the center of a great pile of food and dishes.

You might be thinking, "That was a really long sentence," and you would be right. Long sentences do have a place in good writing. A series of short sentences can become boring and repetitive. Adding a longer sentence with more detail from time to time helps the reader pause and reflect. Your sentences don't have to be as long as mine but you can, and should, write longer sentences sometimes, and it's a good thing to practice.

Now it is your turn.

1. Pick the subject of your sentence and list what information you want to give to your reader.

2. Organize this information to make it easy for your reader to understand it.

3. Write the sentence containing this information in that order.

Step 1: The subject of your sentence and the information you want to give to your reader:

(Subject)_____

(Information)_____

_____

_____

CONTINUED ON NEXT PAGE ➜

Step 2: List by number the pieces of information you have written for step 1.

1. _____

2. _____

3. _____

4. _____

5. _____

Reorder this list so you can give your reader this information in the most interesting or understandable way.

1. _____

2. _____

3. _____

4. _____

5. _____

Today you will write out your sentence. Before you do, let's look at two different ways to write a long sentence.

Compound sentences join together two (or more) simple sentences that have equal and related thoughts. A common way to write a compound sentence is to separate each thought with a comma and add a **coordinating conjunction** *(for, and, nor, but, or, yet, so)* to connect them. Here is an example:

> I enjoyed smelling the cookies while they baked, **but** I'm on a diet and cannot have sweets.

Notice that both of these thoughts could stand alone as a sentence.

> I enjoyed smelling the cookies while they baked.
> I'm on a diet and cannot have sweets.

Both sentences were related and of equal importance, so it was easy to join them with the coordinating conjunction, *but*. (The comma always goes before the conjunction in a compound sentence.)

Complex sentences are similar in that they also join two or more related thoughts into one sentence, but only one of these thoughts can stand alone as a sentence. This type of sentence uses **subordinating conjunctions** instead of coordinating conjunctions because part of the sentence depends on the other part in order to make sense. Examples of subordinating conjunctions are words like **although, because, since, while, after, even though, until, whereas**. You don't need to remember all of the subordinating conjunctions, there are too many of them, but it is helpful to know that if it's a conjunction, and not one of the FANBOYS, then it is subordinating. Here is an example of a complex sentence.

> **Even though** they smelled delicious, I didn't eat any cookies.

Notice that only one of these thoughts could stand alone as a sentence.

> I didn't eat any cookies.

> (*Even though they smelled delicious* is not a complete sentence.)

It's easy to make a complex sentence even longer. I could easily have done this by adding another subordinating conjunction. You can do this lots of times in the same sentence.

> **Even though** they smelled delicious, and **even though** they were warm from the oven, I didn't eat any cookies **because** I am on a diet.

See how easy it can be to write long sentences?

HINT! It would be a great idea to either memorize the coordinating conjunctions or keep a list of them handy. They are pretty easy to remember when you realize they spell the word FANBOYS.

For
And
Nor
But
Or
Yet
So

HINT! A conjunction is a word that connects one thought to another.

CONTINUED ON NEXT PAGE ➔

Step 3: Write your sentence including all the information in the list on the previous page. Be sure to give this information in the order listed.

Don't worry about whether to write a complex or a compound sentence, just write the best sentence you can, then show it to your teacher.

Your sentence:_____

_____

_____

_____

_____

Rewrite your sentence using your teacher's suggestions:

_____

_____

_____

_____

Now you get a chance to show off a little bit. Follow the example page:

1. Write your name and the date in the upper right corner and skip two spaces.

2. Write a title on the first line. You might use for a title "One Perfect Sentence." (Do not use quotation marks around your title.)

3. Skip a line after the title and write your sentence.

4. Skip a line after your sentence and write a brief explanation of how you wrote this perfect sentence. (Use the directions in this exercise to help you organize your explanation.)

5. Give your paper to your teacher.

HINT! Run-on sentences occur when two (or more) complete sentences are connected without proper punctuation, and they should be avoided. Refer to the Helpful Terms section in the back of this book for help with this topic.

CONTINUED ON NEXT PAGE ➜

Your paper should be set up like this example page. Use the worksheet on the next page for this assignment.

Your Name

The Date

SPACE

SPACE

Your Title

SPACE

Your perfect sentence

The end of your sentence

SPACE

The process you used to write this perfect sentence

CONTINUED ON NEXT PAGE➔

How a Sentence Does It
Worksheet

_____

_____

_____

_____

_____

_____

_____

_____

_____

_____

_____

_____

_____

_____

_____

_____

_____

_____

_____

_____

_____

_____

Fill out the "Student Progress Report" on the next page.

Remember to fill out the writing skills mastery check-off form and, if necessary, to record spelling words and other problems that you need to address in the future.

Student Progress Report

This is the best sentence I wrote this week:

_____

_____

_____

_____

I think it is the best because:

_____

_____

_____

_____

I made this mistake this week, and this is what I learned to help me avoid making the mistake again:

_____

_____

_____

_____

This is the sentence showing how I fixed this mistake:

_____

_____

_____

_____

Comments:

_____

_____

_____

_____

Your teacher will assign a book for you to read this week. Be sure to finish it before the end of the week. Review the five steps of reading literature and prepare to describe each of the five elements from your book.

Name of the book: _____

Author of the book: _____

Read and discuss with your teacher

A story is a series of events which may be either fictional or real. Stories are part of our everyday lives. You hear or read about them in books, on television, on the internet, and in conversations. The best way to communicate a story, especially in writing, is by using a literary device called a plot. The plot is how you tell the story.

People have been telling stories since ancient times. In ancient Greece, a writer named Aristotle believed that a story's plot needed to have one main action that was the focus without anything extra. He also believed that a story needed to have a beginning, a middle, and an end.

In many ways, people still write plots that are similar to what Aristotle talked about in ancient Greece. Most stories still do have a recognizable beginning, middle, and end. We usually divide a plot into more elements than this now, which you will learn later in the year, but those divisions are still based on the idea that a story has a beginning, a middle, and an end.

Stories also usually have a main plot, which is the basic story that is being told. It may have additional subplots, which are smaller stories that are also happening. Aristotle probably wouldn't like a story with a lot of subplots, but they are almost always related to the main plot in some way.

A lot of people think about the plot as just being about what happens. However, there is more to plot than that. In a good story, the plot, the characters, and the theme all work together. The theme is the story's message. A good plot will help convey the theme. The plot also makes it easier for the reader to understand the characters because it lets the audience see how the characters respond to what is happening. We'll learn more about these things throughout the rest of the year.

Discussion Questions

Think about one of your favorite stories. What is its plot? Does the story have a beginning, a middle, and an end? What is happening in the beginning? What is happening in the middle? What is happening in the end? Does the story have any subplots? How do you know they are subplots but not the main plot? How does the plot connect with the story's message? What does the plot tell you about the characters?

Objectives:

❶ Learn the basics of plot in literature.

❷ Read the assigned Bible passage.

❸ Answer questions about the assigned Bible passage.

❹ Write a paragraph summary of a plot and then condense into one sentence.

❺ Read and discuss the assigned book (teacher's choice).

HINT! ⸘ When you are telling or writing a story, it is up to you how to organize the elements of that story into a plot.

Read and discuss assigned passage

Read the following passage: Genesis 3:1–24

Step One: Who is this passage about, and what is the cultural and historical setting?

_____

_____

_____

Step Two: What is the genre of this passage (history, poetry, prophecy, proverbs, letters, parables, etc.)?

_____

_____

_____

Step Three: What is the intended meaning of this passage? Some questions you can ask to help with this question are "What fallen or sinful condition is being highlighted in this passage?" or "What prompted the author to write this passage?" (Is this message about sin, salvation, faith, hope, etc.?)

_____

_____

_____

Step Four: Can you list other Bible passages that help define the intended meaning? (A concordance would be helpful here.)

_____

_____

_____

Step Five: Once the original meaning is understood, seek to find a simple life application.

_____

_____

_____

Read and discuss with your teacher

Answer the following questions about the passage:

1. What is the plot of this account (what are the events that happen)?

_____

_____

_____

_____

_____

2. Does the story have a recognizable beginning, middle, and end?
   How do you know?

_____

_____

_____

_____

_____

3. How does the plot connect with the story's theme? If you are not
   sure of what the story's theme is, think about the story's message.
   Does the plot connect to the message in some way?

_____

_____

_____

_____

_____

Complete the following activity

Write a paragraph describing what happened in the Bible passage you read for this week. Be sure to include each main event.

_____

_____

_____

_____

_____

_____

_____

_____

_____

_____

_____

Then, identify the most important information in the paragraph above that is essential to understanding the story. Use letters to identify the most important things in your paragraph.

Next, list each of these items (with the letter you assigned them). Figure out how to organize them and then write them in one sentence. Make sure you use the letters to identify them in the sentence.

_____

_____

_____

_____

_____

_____

_____

Read and discuss assigned book

Remember to keep in mind these five principles when reading the book of your choice this week:

Step One: Determine the genre of the literature (historical fiction, fantasy, drama, Western, mystery, science fiction, poetry, biography, etc.).

_____

_____

_____

Step Two: Read the book, keeping in mind the main setting of the text and the primary roles of each character.

_____

_____

_____

Step Three: Look for the flow of the story. Describe the flow of the story from your book.

_____

_____

_____

Step Four: What is the book's message or what do you think it is trying to teach you?

_____

_____

_____

Step Five: Does this message agree with what the Bible teaches? Why or why not?

_____

_____

_____

Prewriting

The information in your writing should "flow" from one sentence to another. It is not too hard to write this way. It just takes practice. But that is what this exercise will give you.

Notice in the above paragraph that there is a flow of ideas from the first sentence on through the fourth. I will mark the words that show this flow when I write these sentences again, and you will see how this flow of information works:

The (1) information in your writing should (2) flow from one sentence to another. It is (3) not too hard to write this way. It just (4) takes practice. But that is what this (5) exercise will give you.

As you read through the list below, you will see where in the paragraph this occurs.

1. The first sentence mentions that information should flow.

2. The second sentence says it is not hard to write this way.

3. The third sentence says that it just takes practice.

4. The fourth sentence says that this exercise will give you that practice.

Notice that there is an idea connecting each sentence to the next.

Here is another paragraph with flow in its sentences. This time you will chart the flow of ideas just as I did in the last paragraph.

(Sentence 1) Over **ninety percent** of all of the **life forms** that have ever lived in this world **no longer exist**. (2) This is **not all bad** for us. (3) There have been **things alive** that we would **not like to meet** or have live near us. (4) Some creatures were very **large meat-eaters** who would have liked nothing better than **to have had us over for lunch**. (5) Think of **sharks** that were **sixty feet long, meat-eating animals as tall as a four-story building,** or **snakes fifty feet long**. (6) We might even **be better off** today because **some species are no longer with us**.

Objectives:

❶ Ideas in sentences can be connected.

❷ Ideas can flow from one sentence to the next.

❸ You can make ideas in your writing flow from one point to another.

CONTINUED ON NEXT PAGE➜

Writing

Chart the flow of ideas in that paragraph by listing the main idea of each sentence. I have made bold the main ideas (bits of information) in each sentence. (In some cases there is a separation between the bits.)

First sentence: _____

Second sentence: _____

Third sentence: _____

Fourth sentence: _____

Fifth sentence: _____

Sixth sentence: _____

We can even create flowing sentences if we do this process backwards. This time I will write the ideas, and you will write the sentences. Together we will make the ideas flow from one sentence to the next.

You are to write six sentences based on the following six ideas.

1. Bill's pet

2. Not big

3. Carried it

4. Got away

5. Mother found it

6. Surprised mom

Write your six sentences. Each of your sentences should contain the bit of information that is numbered for that sentence.

For example: 1. Bill's pet. You should make this into a sentence that tells your reader that Bill had a pet and what it was.

Of course, the sentences you write will be longer than the bits in the list. In 1, the bit of information says that Bill had a pet. That information is not a sentence and you will have to add to it. Yours might say something like this: Bill Jones found a snake and thought it would make a nice pet. (Think of a new sentence about a pet. Do not use my sentence.)

So, when you write sentence number one, use my words, *Bill* and *pet*, then use your own words for the rest of the sentence. Do the same for the other sentences.

1. _____

   _____

2. _____

   _____

3. _____

   _____

4. _____

   _____

5. _____

   _____

6. _____

   _____

You can do this next part of this exercise without as much help. Write a paragraph that is built on the same steps you used to write those sentences. Describe some simple action that you do well. Start in the first sentence with the first thing you do. The second sentence will tell the second thing you do, and so on.

Be very careful that there is a flow from one bit of information in each sentence to the next sentence. As an example of how to do this, I will tell you about how good a cook I am.

I am good at making peanut butter sandwiches. Below is a paragraph that has flow that tells how I make a peanut butter sandwich. Notice that the sentences have, as main ideas, the steps I use to make the sandwich. These steps and sentences come in the same order. This means that the first thing I do to make a sandwich is in the first sentence and the second thing I do to make the sandwich is in the second sentence, and so on.

1. Materials   2. Knife and plate

3. Open jar and bread   4. Spread butter and peanut butter

5. Put sides together   6. Enjoy eating it

Here are these bits of information presented in a paragraph. Notice how the information in this paragraph flows from one sentence to the next one:

> When I make a peanut butter sandwich, the first thing I do is (1) gather all of the materials I will need: the peanut butter, butter, and bread. Of course, I have to have a (2) plate and a knife. After I have all of these things on the counter, I open the (3) jar and the bread package. The best part, the one I like the best, is (4) spreading the butter and the peanut butter on one side of one of the pieces of bread. Putting the (5) slices of bread together is the last step. Oh, yes, I almost forgot, I get to (6) enjoy eating the sandwich I made.

You probably cannot cook as well as I can, so you will have to think of something that you know how to do. You can write about how you ride a bike, work with your computer, hem a dress, program the TV, wash dishes, train your horse, or anything else that you are very good at.

Make a list of the steps you take to do this activity. Make sure that the order of the steps makes sense.

_____

_____

_____

_____

_____

_____

_____

_____

_____

_____

_____

_____

_____

_____

_____

_____

_____

_____

_____

_____

_____

Turn your list into a paragraph in which the ideas flow from one sentence to the next.

HINT! If your sentences do not flow beautifully, do not worry about it. Soon they will.

_____

_____

_____

_____

_____

_____

_____

_____

_____

_____

_____

_____

_____

_____

_____

_____

_____

_____

_____

Fill out the "Student Progress Report" on the next page.

Remember to fill out the writing skills mastery check-off form and, if necessary, to record spelling words and other problems that you need to address in the future.

Student Progress Report

This is the best sentence I wrote this week:

_____

_____

_____

_____

I think it is the best because:

_____

_____

_____

_____

I made this mistake this week, and this is what I learned to help me avoid making the mistake again:

_____

_____

_____

_____

This is the sentence showing how I fixed this mistake:

_____

_____

_____

_____

Comments:

_____

_____

_____

_____

Your teacher will assign a book for you to read this week. Be sure to finish it before the end of the week. Review the five steps of reading literature and prepare to describe each of the five elements from your book.

Name of the book: _____

Author of the book: _____

Read and discuss with your teacher

One of the best ways to be sure you understand what is going on in the plot is to make sure you understand the sequence of events and how those events connect.

Many plots are chronological. That means that events are told in the order that they happened. But many other plots are not chronological. Sometimes plots include flashbacks, which jump back to an event in the past, or they have flashforwards, which jump ahead to an event that has not happened yet. It can be confusing to follow what is happening if you do not understand that the events are not being told in sequence.

Discussion Questions

Think about some of your favorite stories. Are the events in chronological order or are they given out of order? How do you know? Do you prefer one over the other?

Objectives:

❶ Learn about the importance of sequence of events in plot.

❷ Read the assigned Bible passage.

❸ Answer questions about the assigned Bible passage.

❹ Arrange events into the right sequence.

❺ Write a summary of the events that happened that flows well and is in the right order.

❻ Read and discuss the assigned book (teacher's choice).

HINT! ⸜ Flashbacks jump back to an event in the past, while flashforwards jump ahead to an event that has not happened yet.

Read and discuss assigned passage

Read the following Bible passage: Genesis 22:1–19

Step One: Who is this passage about, and what is the cultural and historical setting?

_____

_____

_____

Step Two: What is the genre of this passage (history, poetry, prophecy, proverbs, letters, parables, etc.)?

_____

_____

_____

Step Three: What is the intended meaning of this passage? Some questions you can ask to help with this question are "What fallen or sinful condition is being highlighted in this passage?" or "What prompted the author to write this passage?" (Is this message about sin, salvation, faith, hope, etc.?)

_____

_____

_____

Step Four: Can you list other Bible passages that help define the intended meaning? (A concordance would be helpful here.)

_____

_____

_____

Step Five: Once the original meaning is understood, seek to find a simple life application.

_____

_____

_____

Read and discuss with your teacher

Answer the following questions about the passage:

1. What is the plot of this story (what are the events that happen)?

_____

_____

_____

2. Does the story have a recognizable beginning, middle, and end? How do you know?

_____

_____

_____

3. How does the plot connect with the story's theme? If you are not sure of what the story's theme is, think about the story's message. Does the plot connect to the message in some way?

_____

_____

_____

Complete the following activity

Unscramble the order of events in the Bible passage and put them in the right order. Now write a paragraph that includes all of these events but make sure that you add words to help the sentences flow well.

_____ God blessed Abraham.

_____ God told Abraham to sacrifice Isaac at Mt. Moriah.

_____ Abraham said that God will provide.

_____ God decided to test Abraham.

_____ Abraham raised the knife to sacrifice Isaac.

_____ God provided a ram.

_____ Abraham and Isaac traveled to Beersheba.

_____ Isaac asked where the lamb was.

_____ God stopped Abraham.

_____ Abraham sacrificed the ram.

_____ Abraham and Isaac traveled to Mt. Moriah.

_____

_____

_____

_____

_____

_____

_____

_____

_____

_____

_____

_____

_____

_____

Read and discuss assigned book

Remember to keep in mind these five principles when reading the book of your choice this week:

Step One: Determine the genre of the literature (historical fiction, fantasy, drama, Western, mystery, science fiction, poetry, biography, etc.).

_____

_____

_____

Step Two: Read the book, keeping in mind the main setting of the text and the primary roles of each character.

_____

_____

_____

Step Three: Look for the flow of the story. Describe the flow of the story from your book.

_____

_____

_____

Step Four: What is the book's message or what do you think it is trying to teach you?

_____

_____

_____

Step Five: Does this message agree with what the Bible teaches? Why or why not?

_____

_____

_____

Prewriting

An author builds a story out of ideas and actions. It is possible to find the main ideas or actions in a story you read and then write about them. This is called writing a synopsis or summary. When you write a story summary you do not need to talk about everything that happens in the story, but you do need to cover the main story elements:

Setting (Time And Place)

This is the time and the place in which the story occurs. Some stories you read have pictures. Pictures can give you clues as to the time and place of the story. Ask your teacher to select a story with pictures, and together you can decide what you can tell about the time and place from the pictures. Look for things like:

a. Style of clothing
c. Types of trees
e. Machinery

b. Weather conditions
d. Landscape
f. Tools

There should also be word clues about the time and place. The characters may talk about and use many things that will tell you about when and where the story takes place. If you ask, your teacher may help you pick out some of these.

Characters

The characters are the people in the story. The main character or characters of your stories will be introduced to you by the authors early in the stories. There may be information about:

a. Their age and physical characteristics
b. Whether they are male or female
c. Their relationship to other characters
d. Their personality and motivations

Conflict

The main character or characters will have a goal. They will want something or will want to do something. They may want to capture wild horses, build rafts, climb mountains, make dinner, or the characters may face problems, such as how to find the way home or how to survive a flood. In most stories, there will be forces that will try to keep the main characters from getting what they want. These may be natural forces like gravity or winter weather. They may be other people like teachers or neighbors or cruel neighborhood bullies. The force could even be a weakness of the main character. As the main character(s) faces these forces, the story builds to a climax, which results in a turning point in the story.

Objectives:

❶ Recognize the main points in a story.

❷ List the main points in your summary of a story.

HINT! If you look at these story parts one at a time, it will make it easier for you to find them in your reading.

HINT! We will talk more about the main parts of a story in future lessons.

CONTINUED ON NEXT PAGE➜

Resolution

After the turning point, the action in the story declines as you near the resolution. This is when you find out who wins or who loses, or whether the main character(s) achieved their goal, and all the loose ends of the story are wrapped up.

Ask your teacher to select a story for you to read. You are going to write a summary paper that tells what the story is about. Think about the different story parts as you read. Tomorrow you will create an outline for your paper.

HINT! Pay attention to the setting, characters, and conflict as you read this story.

The Main Points
Outline

Writing

Now that you have read the story you can list the main parts on this outline. It's okay if you need to look at the book again to help you remember.

Title of Book: _____

Author of Book: _____

When: _____

Where: _____

Who: _____ a. _____ Age: _____

    Kind of Person: _____ _____

Who: _____ b. _____ Age: _____

    Kind of Person: _____ _____

Who: _____ c. _____ Age: _____

    Kind of Person: _____ _____

The Conflict: _____

_____

The Force Against: _____

_____

Climax or Turning Point: _____

_____

Resolution: _____

_____

Use your outline to write a paper that tells what the story is about. You can take 2 days to complete this paper. Here is an example of what a book summary should read like. You can see that my book summary has all the main parts.

"To Build a Raft" by Bill Smith takes place in modern times in the northwestern part of the United States (**setting**). John and his friend, Fred, are both about nine years old (**characters**) and would like to build a raft, but they are not allowed to use a chainsaw to cut the logs for it (**conflict**).

They try to make the raft of small logs, but the raft is not big enough to hold them. They try to tie small trees and logs together that are already cut or broken, but they are all different sizes; the raft pulls apart and they fall in the pond (**forces against** and **climax**).

A neighbor has a chainsaw. The boys agree to pile his firewood for him, and he agrees to cut them some logs for their raft. The boys work for the neighbor for two days, and he cuts them enough logs for a raft. They tie these logs together, put up a sail, and have a fine raft (**resolution**).

CONTINUED ON NEXT PAGE➔

Story Summary Worksheet

_____

_____

_____

_____

_____

_____

_____

_____

_____

_____

_____

_____

_____

_____

_____

_____

_____

_____

_____

_____

_____

_____

_____

_____

_____

_____

_____

Continue your paper today.

_____

_____

_____

_____

_____

_____

_____

_____

_____

_____

_____

_____

_____

_____

_____

_____

_____

_____

_____

_____

_____

_____

_____

_____

_____

_____

Fill out the "Student Progress Report" on the next page.

Remember to fill out the writing skills mastery check-off form and, if necessary, to record spelling words and other problems that you need to address in the future.

Student Progress Report

This is the best sentence I wrote this week:

_____

_____

_____

_____

I think it is the best because:

_____

_____

_____

_____

I made this mistake this week, and this is what I learned to help me avoid making the mistake again:

_____

_____

_____

_____

This is the sentence showing how I fixed this mistake:

_____

_____

_____

_____

Comments:

_____

_____

_____

_____

Your teacher will assign a book for you to read this week. Be sure to finish it before the end of the week. Review the five steps of reading literature and prepare to describe each of the five elements from your book.

Name of the book: _____

Author of the book: _____

Read and discuss with your teacher

We've learned how it is important to understand the order of events in the plot. One reason is that it is easier to understand cause and effect in the plot if you know the order that things happen. The cause is "why" something happens, and the effect is the thing that happens.

Connections between events in the plot are easier to understand if you know that one thing caused another or is the result of something else. In my summary example from the last lesson, John and Fred build a raft out of logs that are too small (cause), and end up falling in the pond (effect). If you are having trouble figuring out what caused something, a good way to find out is to keep asking the question "why?"

Discussion Questions

Think about one of your favorite stories. What is one of the things that happens in the plot? What is the cause of this event? What effects does this event lead to?

Objectives:

❶ Learn about the importance of sequence of events in plot.

❷ Read the assigned Bible passage.

❸ Answer questions about the assigned Bible passage.

❹ Write a paragraph.

❺ Read and discuss the assigned book (teacher's choice).

Read and discuss assigned passage

Read the following passage together: Genesis 25:24–34, Genesis 27:1–45

Step One: Who is this passage about, and what is the cultural and historical setting?

_____

_____

_____

Step Two: What is the genre of this passage (history, poetry, prophecy, proverbs, letters, parables, etc.)?

_____

_____

_____

Step Three: What is the intended meaning of this passage? Some questions you can ask to help with this question are "What fallen or sinful condition is being highlighted in this passage?" or "What prompted the author to write this passage?" (Is this message about sin, salvation, faith, hope, etc.?)

_____

_____

_____

Step Four: Can you list other Bible passages that help define the intended meaning? (A concordance would be helpful here.)

_____

_____

_____

Step Five: Once the original meaning is understood, seek to find a simple life application.

_____

_____

_____

Read and discuss with your teacher

Answer the following questions about the passage:

1. What is the plot of this story (what are the events that happen)?

_____

_____

_____

_____

2. Does the story have a recognizable beginning, middle, and end? How do you know?

_____

_____

_____

_____

3. How does the plot connect with the story's theme? If you are not sure of what the story's theme is, think about the story's message. Does the plot connect to the message in some way?

_____

_____

_____

_____

Complete the following activity

In the passage this week, Isaac gives Jacob his blessing. What caused this to happen? What happened because Isaac blessed Jacob instead of Esau? Write a paragraph explaining cause and effect in the passage. Be sure to explain the connection between events clearly.

_____

_____

_____

_____

_____

_____

_____

_____

_____

_____

_____

Read and discuss assigned book

Remember to keep in mind these five principles when reading the book of your choice this week:

Step One: Determine the genre of the literature (historical fiction, fantasy, drama, Western, mystery, science fiction, poetry, biography, etc.).

_____

_____

_____

Step Two: Read the book, keeping in mind the main setting of the text and the primary roles of each character.

_____

_____

_____

Step Three: Look for the flow of the story. Describe the flow of the story from your book.

_____

_____

_____

Step Four: What is the book's message or what do you think it is trying to teach you?

_____

_____

_____

CONTINUED ON NEXT PAGE→

Step Five: Does this message agree with what the Bible teaches? Why or why not?

_____

_____

_____

Writing
Lesson 4

Day 31

I Feel
Description

Name

Prewriting

Sometimes it is hard to talk about how you feel. This exercise will make it easy for you to write about how you felt about something that happened to you.

There are lots of different ways to feel about some other person, a place you have been, or something that has happened to you.

In fact, everything you have ever done has made you feel some way. Every time you go into your house you feel something. When you sit down to dinner you feel. When you walk into a library you have feelings. When you see the check-out lady at the grocery store you feel something about her or about the parent paying for the food.

If you follow the steps below, you will be able to describe how you felt about something so that other people who read what you have written will understand how and why you felt that way.

Writing

There are 4 steps used in describing how you felt about something.

Step 1. You will have to pick an event you have been involved in. It does not have to be an important thing at all. Anything will do.

Step 2. Decide how you felt about this event. Try to write this in one word.

Step 3. List the things you saw, heard, and touched that made you feel that way.

Step 4. Put all of this together in an explanation of how you felt.

I will list these four points to show you how easy this is: (Check the above list as you read this example for how each of the four points works.)

Step 1. (Event) I had to walk to the car in the rain today.

Step 2. (How I felt) First mad, then glad.

Step 3. (What I saw, heard, and touched) I saw, heard, and touched things that changed how I felt.

　　a. I saw water on the car.

　　b. I saw rain falling.

　　c. I heard rain on the roof of the car.

　　d. I saw puddles of water in the driveway.

Objectives:

❶ Decide how you felt about something that happened to you.

❷ Understand that it is possible to explain how you felt about an event.

❸ Describe how you felt about an event.

❹ Practice writing compound sentences.

CONTINUED ON NEXT PAGE➔

e. I felt rain on my face and hands.

f. I could smell the rain.

Step 4. (Put all this together)

At first I was mad when I walked to the car in the rain today but that changed. I knew it was raining when I saw water standing on the finish of the car. The drops hit the metal top with a ping. There were puddles of water standing in the driveway. When I stepped off the porch, I could feel the rain on my face and hands. I could even smell it. It smelled like spring. This made me glad that winter was about over and that spring would soon be here, and when I thought of that, I was no longer mad but was glad that it was raining.

I will take apart this paragraph and label where the pieces of it came from.

(**Topic Sentence**) At first I was mad when I walked to the car in the rain today but that changed.

(**Saw**) I knew it was raining when I saw water standing on the finish of the car.

(**Heard**) The drops hit the metal top with a ping.

(**Saw**) There were puddles of water standing in the driveway.

(**Felt**) When I stepped off the porch, I could feel the rain on my face and hands.

(**Smelled**) I could even smell it. It smelled like spring.

(**How this changed how I felt about the rain**) This made me glad that winter was about over and that spring would soon be here, and when I thought of that, I was no longer mad but was glad that it was raining.

Now you are to do this exercise the same way that I did. Today, you will complete 3 of the 4 steps. Think of something you have experienced in your life and how you felt about it. It doesn't have to be a major event. It can even be how you felt about getting out of bed this morning.

Step 1. (Event) _____

Step 2. (How you felt) _____

Step 3. (List of experiences. Check my list to see how to make your list.)

a. _____

b. _____

c. _____

d. _____

e. _____

Step 4. Now you will finish the last step. Using your answers from yesterday, write a paragraph that puts it all together. Try writing one or more compound or complex sentences in this exercise.

HINT! A compound sentence is two complete sentences joined by a comma and a conjunction. See Lesson 1.

_____

_____

_____

_____

_____

_____

_____

_____

_____

_____

_____

You now have the **body** of a paragraph. You need a topic sentence and then you will have a complete paragraph.

A topic sentence tells the reader what kinds of information will be in the paragraph. You will have to think of a sentence that will tell your reader that you had feelings about something that happened to you.

This topic sentence will be the first sentence in your paragraph. It could say something simple like: *I felt good today*, or *I was embarrassed yesterday*, or *I was glad it was Saturday*. Write your topic sentence for your paragraph.

_____

_____

_____

_____

_____

HINT! A **topic sentence** tells the reader what kinds of information will be in the paragraph.

Put the pieces of your paragraph together on the Description Worksheet.

Set your paper up this way: Your **name** and **date** in the upper right corner. **Skip two spaces**. Write a **title** for your paper on the first line of the page. Make it simple like, I Feel. **Skip one line** and write your **paragraph** starting with your **topic sentence**. Check this example paper outline.

Your Name

The Date

SPACE

SPACE

Your Title

SPACE

Your paragraph (indent the topic sentence)

CONTINUED ON NEXT PAGE →

Description Worksheet

_____

_____

_____

_____

_____

_____

_____

_____

_____

_____

_____

_____

_____

_____

_____

_____

_____

_____

_____

_____

_____

_____

_____

Fill out the "Student Progress Report" on the next page.

Remember to fill out the writing skills mastery check-off form and, if necessary, to record spelling words and other problems that you need to address in the future.

CONTINUED ON NEXT PAGE➔

Student Progress Report

This is the best sentence I wrote this week:

_____

_____

_____

_____

I think it is the best because:

_____

_____

_____

_____

I made this mistake this week, and this is what I learned to help me avoid making the mistake again:

_____

_____

_____

_____

This is the sentence showing how I fixed this mistake:

_____

_____

_____

_____

Comments:

_____

_____

_____

_____

Your teacher will assign a book for you to read this week. Be sure to finish it before the end of the week. Review the five steps of reading literature and prepare to describe each of the five elements from your book.

Name of the book: _____

Author of the book: _____

Read and discuss with your teacher

We don't just study plot to know what is happening in a story. The plot itself helps us understand the characters better because we get to see how a character responds to events. Any sort of event can provide a way for us to see the characters in action. Even a scene that is just a discussion around the dinner table will provide the reader with a way to gain insight into the characters. A timid character may not say anything, while a forceful character may dominate the discussion and decide on a plan of action.

Likewise, the story about a journey would also provide a lot of insight into the characters, depending on how they acted during different points of the plot. If the characters get lost, how do they respond to this situation? One character might try to find help while another might sit down and cry. Another character might try to comfort the one who is crying while yet another complains about being lost.

All these characters are in the same situation, but they all respond differently. How they respond to the plot tells you a lot about them — the one who tries to find help is probably very resourceful or determined. The one who is crying might be easily upset or frightened, and the one who is trying to calm that character is probably kind. The one who is complaining might be hard to please.

Sometimes, the plot just affects the characters. They do not really change the direction of the story. Instead, they just react to what happens. In the case of the people on the journey, they might travel the whole way and the plot could just consist of them reacting to various challenges they face, like bad weather or difficult people.

More often, characters actively affect the plot. For instance, perhaps one of the characters on the journey decides to stop traveling and instead help out a city that is in need of help. That would change the direction of the story. Main characters are more likely to affect the plot than supporting characters, though they don't always get to do that.

Discussion Questions

Think about one of your favorite stories. Who is the main character? What is the plot of the story? Does the plot help you understand the character more? Why or why not? Does this character affect the plot or does the character just react to what is happening?

Objectives:

❶ Learn about the important connection between character and plot.

❷ Read the assigned Bible passage.

❸ Answer questions about the assigned Bible passage.

❹ Write a paragraph.

❺ Read and discuss the assigned book (teacher's choice).

Read and discuss assigned passage

Read the following Bible passage: Genesis 37:1–36

Step One: Who is this passage about, and what is the cultural and historical setting?

_____

_____

_____

Step Two: What is the genre of this passage (history, poetry, prophecy, proverbs, letters, parables, etc.)?

_____

_____

_____

Step Three: What is the intended meaning of this passage? Some questions you can ask to help with this question are "What fallen or sinful condition is being highlighted in this passage?" or "What prompted the author to write this passage?" (Is this message about sin, salvation, faith, hope, etc.?)

_____

_____

_____

Step Four: Can you list other Bible passages that help define the intended meaning? (A concordance would be helpful here.)

_____

_____

_____

Step Five: Once the original meaning is understood, seek to find a simple life application.

_____

_____

_____

Read and discuss with your teacher

Answer the following questions about the passage:

1. What is the plot of this story (what are the events that happen)?

_____

_____

_____

2. Does the story have a recognizable beginning, middle, and end?
   How do you know?

_____

_____

_____

3. How does the plot connect with the story's theme? If you are not
   sure of what the story's theme is, think about the story's message.
   Does the plot connect to the message in some way?

_____

_____

_____

Complete the following activity

In the passage you read this week, there are a few different characters whose actions and words are detailed. We see Joseph interact with his brothers. We also see how Reuben and Judah react to Joseph's situation compared with the other brothers, and we also see how Jacob reacts to the news.

Pick one of these characters and write a paragraph about what his actions in the plot reveal about that character. Be sure to include a topic sentence, and make sure your sentences flow well between each other.

_____

_____

_____

_____

_____

_____

_____

_____

_____

_____

_____

_____

CONTINUED ON NEXT PAGE ➜

Read and discuss assigned book

Remember to keep in mind these five principles when reading the book of your choice this week:

Step One: Determine the genre of the literature (historical fiction, fantasy, drama, Western, mystery, science fiction, poetry, biography, etc.).

_____

_____

_____

Step Two: Read the book, keeping in mind the main setting of the text and the primary roles of each character.

_____

_____

_____

Step Three: Look for the flow of the story. Describe the flow of the story from your book.

_____

_____

_____

Step Four: What is the book's message or what do you think it is trying to teach you?

_____

_____

_____

CONTINUED ON NEXT PAGE➔

Step Five: Does this message agree with what the Bible teaches? Why or why not?

_____

_____

_____

Prewriting

We all make mistakes. It is how we learn. If we did not make mistakes, we would not learn. This week you will analyze a mistake you made and write a paper about your mistake.

Here are the steps you will use to write this paper:

1. **Name a mistake** you have made.

2. **List the actions** that led to the mistake.

3. **Decide** which actions caused the mistake.

4. Figure out what you **could have done** to avoid the mistake.

5. **Describe the changes** you will make in your actions so you will not make that same mistake again.

I did this exercise for a mistake I made. I numbered the above points in the paragraph so you could see how they fit. I labeled the topic sentence **(TS)**.

> **(TS) Last night I made a mistake as I was helping my wife do the dishes.** I carried the dishes from the table to the counter. When I piled the dinner plates on the counter, **(1) I did not take the silverware off the plates** first. This made the plates wobbly. **(2)** When I put the **fourth plate on the stack** on the counter and turned back for another load, the top **plate slipped** off the pile and broke on the floor. **(3)** It was **leaving the knives and forks on the plates that** caused them to tip off the counter. **(4)** They **should have been taken off each plate** as it was stacked. **(5)** If my wife lets me help her do the dishes again, **I will put the silverware to one side when I stack the plates.**

Objectives:

❶ Admit that you did something that was a mistake.

❷ Analyze what you did.

❸ Recognize the action that caused the mistake.

Writing

Make a short list of mistakes you have made sometime in the past.

1. _____

2. _____

3. _____

Ask your teacher to look at this list and help you pick out a mistake that would be easy for you to analyze. Make a list of the actions that you took in making that mistake. This list does not need to be in sentences. Use words or phrases if you want to; my list looked like this:

1. Carried pile of dishes to counter

2. Did not remove silverware

3. Piled plates on each other with silverware on them

List the actions that led to your mistake similar to the listing above.

1. _____

2. _____

3. _____

A compound sentence joins two or more sentences together; they consist of at least two related thoughts.

Earlier in this course you practiced writing compound sentence using a comma and a conjunction. You can also make a compound sentence with a semicolon (see the first sentence above). You do not use a conjunction when using a semicolon. Notice the difference in the sentences below.

Bill took a taxi; Sally walked home.

Bill took a taxi, but Sally walked home.

Both of these sentences work. Practice writing a compound sentence with a semicolon in this exercise.

Turn yesterday's list of actions into complete sentences. One of your sentences should be a compound sentence.

1. _____

_____

_____

2. _____

_____

_____

3. _____

_____

_____

Now think of a topic sentence that tells your reader what your paragraph is about. It can be like mine when I wrote that I made a mistake when I was helping my wife. Write your topic sentence here:

_____

_____

_____

Now figure out what you could have done to avoid the mistake you made and make a note of that here:

_____

_____

_____

Think about what you can do in the future to avoid making the same mistake and make a note of that here:

_____

_____

_____

Tomorrow you will put all this together in your paper on the My Mistake Worksheet. Try to use at least one compound sentence in your final paper.

Below is a chart showing what this paper should look like when you are finished. Write your paper on the My Mistake Worksheet.

Your Name

The Date

SPACE

SPACE

Your Title

SPACE

List of Actions Causing Mistake

1.

2.

3.

4.

Action List Turned Into Sentences

1.

2.

3.

4.

Topic sentence for the paragraph (Indent your topic sentence.):

CONTINUED ON NEXT PAGE➜

My Mistake Worksheet

_____

_____

_____

_____

_____

_____

_____

_____

_____

_____

_____

_____

_____

_____

_____

_____

_____

_____

_____

_____

_____

_____

Fill out the "Student Progress Report" on the next page.

Remember to fill out the writing skills mastery check-off form and, if necessary, to record spelling words and other problems that you need to address in the future.

Student Progress Report

This is the best sentence I wrote this week:

_____

_____

_____

_____

I think it is the best because:

_____

_____

_____

_____

I made this mistake this week, and this is what I learned to help me
avoid making the mistake again:

_____

_____

_____

_____

This is the sentence showing how I fixed this mistake:

_____

_____

_____

_____

Comments:

_____

_____

_____

_____

Your teacher will assign a book for you to read this week. Be sure to finish it before the end of the week. Review the five steps of reading literature and prepare to describe each of the five elements from your book.

Name of the book: _____

Author of the book: _____

Read and discuss with your teacher

There are two main types of stories: plot-driven and character-driven.

Plot-driven stories focus more on the events of the plot — the action of the story, the events that happen. These types of stories can be very fun and are usually fast-paced. For that reason, they easily can hold a reader's attention.

Character-driven stories focus far more on the characters. These stories are less about action happening outside of the character and more about what is going on inside the character — his or her thoughts and feelings and how the character changes throughout the course of the story. These stories usually are not as action-packed, but they can be very interesting and engaging.

Stories very rarely are only plot-driven or only character-driven. A plot-driven story with no character development results in a reader who is not emotionally connected to the characters and therefore may lose interest in what is happening in the plot. A character-driven story with no plot is just as unsatisfying because there is nothing for the characters to do, and there is therefore, no reason to be drawn into the characters' experiences.

Discussion Questions

Think about your favorite story. What would you say is the primary driving force — plot or character? Why do you think that? Do you still see the other driving force at work in the story? If so, where? Based on your readings, do you think you prefer plot-driven stories or character-driven stories? Why?

Objectives:

❶ Learn about the different types of driving forces in story plots.

❷ Read the assigned Bible passage.

❸ Answer questions about the assigned Bible passage.

❹ Write a paragraph.

❺ Read and discuss the assigned book (teacher's choice).

HINT! ⩶ Plot-driven stories focus more on the events of the plot. Character-driven stories focus far more on the characters.

Read and discuss assigned passage

Read the following Bible passage together: Exodus 3:1–4:20

Step One: Who is this passage about, and what is the cultural and historical setting?

_____

_____

_____

Step Two: What is the genre of this passage (history, poetry, prophecy, proverbs, letters, parables, etc.)?

_____

_____

_____

Step Three: What is the intended meaning of this passage? Some questions you can ask to help with this question are "What fallen or sinful condition is being highlighted in this passage?" or "What prompted the author to write this passage?" (Is this message about sin, salvation, faith, hope, etc.?)

_____

_____

_____

Step Four: Can you list other Bible passages that help define the intended meaning? (A concordance would be helpful here.)

_____

_____

_____

Step Five: Once the original meaning is understood, seek to find a simple life application.

_____

_____

_____

Read and discuss with your teacher

Answer the following questions about the passage:

1. What is the plot of this story (what are the events that happen)?

_____

_____

_____

2. Does the story have a recognizable beginning, middle, and end? How do you know?

_____

_____

_____

3. How does the plot connect with the story's theme? If you are not sure of what the story's theme is, think about the story's message. Does the plot connect to the message in some way?

_____

_____

_____

Complete the following activity

Do you think the story of Moses and the burning bush is plot-driven or character-driven? Why do you think this? Write a paragraph where you argue for one or the other. Be sure to use specific examples, to include a topic sentence at the beginning, and to have your sentences flow well between each other.

_____

_____

_____

_____

_____

_____

_____

_____

_____

_____

_____

_____

_____

Read and discuss assigned book

Remember to keep in mind these five principles when reading the book of your choice this week:

Step One: Determine the genre of the literature (historical fiction, fantasy, drama, Western, mystery, science fiction, poetry, biography, etc.).

_____

_____

_____

Step Two: Read the book, keeping in mind the main setting of the text and the primary roles of each character.

_____

_____

_____

Step Three: Look for the flow of the story. Describe the flow of the story from your book.

_____

_____

_____

Step Four: What is the book's message or what do you think it is trying to teach you?

_____

_____

_____

Step Five: Does this message agree with what the Bible teaches? Why or why not?

_____

_____

_____

Prewriting

Writers must talk to their readers because that is what writing is all about; however, a writer cannot speak directly to any reader. This voice must come from the pages of writing. This voice that writers create is called the *narrative voice*. The writer writes the words on the page, but the real teller of the story is the narrative voice who says the words to the reader.

The narrative voice can take different forms, and writers must choose which form they want to use in their story. There are three different narrative voices that an author can choose: **first person, second person**, and **third person**.

First Person:

When the narrative voice is in first person, the narrator is a character in the story and will use pronouns like I, me, and myself. First person sounds like this:

> I saw the dog that had been lost by the rich man. I wanted to make sure he got his dog back and that I got the reward.

It is important to understand that when using first person in a story, the narrator cannot know what other characters are thinking. This is because characters are not mind readers. This narrative voice can tell the reader what he or she is thinking, but that is all this character/voice can tell about what is going on in anyone's mind.

Third Person:

When the narrative voice is not a character in the story, it is called third person. This voice sounds like it is standing outside of the story looking in, and it tells the reader what happens to the people in the story. The third person voice uses pronouns like *he, she, they*, and *them*. Third person sounds like this:

> Bill found the dog that had been lost by the rich man. He wanted to collect the reward, so he made sure the man got his dog back.

What I want you to understand is that there are two main narrative voices: first person and third person, and they work differently. (The **second person** voice is rarely used in literature, but we will learn a little about it in the next lesson.)

Objectives:

❶ Understand that writers create voices which speak to their readers.

❷ Understand that all the voices writers use do not work in the same way.

❸ Understand that writers must choose a voice to talk to their reader.

CONTINUED ON NEXT PAGE➔

You will start a very short story about a dog and its trainer. You will have to tell your reader what the dog is thinking. You will not be able to tell your reader what the man is thinking because you will be using the first person voice to tell the story. (This character/narrative voice will be the voice of the dog.)

I will start the story for you. Your job will be to finish the story using first person. This narrative voice has no way of knowing what is in the man's mind.

> When the man brought **me** home from the pound, **I** realized there was a lot he had to learn. He knew almost nothing about how to treat dogs.
>
> At first **I** thought that it would be easy to train him, but, after the second day, **I** knew **I** had a real job on **my** paws. One of the first things **I** had to teach him was when to let **me** out. He was a very slow learner. **I** did not want to do it, but sometimes **I** even had to scratch on the door to get him to act right.
>
> Another problem **I** had was teaching him about fresh water. . . .

Writing

Use your imagination to finish this short story about training the dog owner. Begin by completing the paragraph about fresh water, then add an ending. Remember, you are writing this in first person.

You **must stay in first person**, and the **narrative voice** must remain **limited** to what **the dog/character/narrative voice** could know.

_____

_____

_____

_____

_____

_____

_____

_____

_____

_____

_____

_____

_____

_____

_____

_____

Today you are going to practice writing with a narrative voice that is **not a character** in the story.

Here is how I rewrote the same passage in third person. I have bolded the use of **third person**.

The day **the man** brought **the dog** home from the pound it looked like **they** would get along fine. But later that evening the trouble started. **The dog** began to scratch on the door. **The man** thought to himself, "He just came in. He cannot have to go out already." **The man** figured that if **he** just ignored the dog, **it** would forget about going out. **He** did not know that is not how it is with dogs.

The dog thought that the man would never learn to deal with **a dog** the way he should.

Now it's your turn. Read the first part of the story again (from Day 51) and change it from first person to third person. Use your own words.

_____

_____

_____

_____

_____

_____

_____

_____

_____

_____

_____

_____

_____

Today you will finish telling the story about the man and the dog in third person by adding to what you wrote yesterday. Write your complete paper on the Dog Story Worksheet.

Your Name

The Date

SPACE

SPACE

Your Title

SPACE

First person voice

Third person voice

CONTINUED ON NEXT PAGE→

Dog Story Worksheet

When you are done with your story, define the following terms for your teacher to demonstrate that you are learning good stuff. First, talk to your teacher about the differences in the narrative voices in each story. Then read your two stories out loud.

Be sure to use the words below when you talk about the differences in the two narrative voices. Go over the following five points. Start by describing what a narrative voice does.

1. **Narrative voice:** What is a narrative voice and what are the two kinds used in the two stories?

2. **First person:** What does first person sound like and what can it not talk about?

3. **Third person:** What does third person sound like and what can it talk about?

Fill out the "Student Progress Report" on the next page.

Remember to fill out the writing skills mastery check-off form and, if necessary, to record spelling words and other problems that you need to address in the future.

CONTINUED ON NEXT PAGE➔

Student Progress Report

This is the best sentence I wrote this week:

_____

_____

_____

_____

I think it is the best because:

_____

_____

_____

_____

I made this mistake this week, and this is what I learned to help me
avoid making the mistake again:

_____

_____

_____

_____

This is the sentence showing how I fixed this mistake:

_____

_____

_____

_____

Comments:

_____

_____

_____

_____

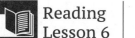
Your teacher will assign a book for you to read this week. Be sure to finish it before the end of the week. Review the five steps of reading literature and prepare to describe each of the five elements from your book.

Name of the book: _____

Author of the book: _____

Read and discuss with your teacher

Do you remember when we talked about plots having beginnings and middles and endings? That was what ancient Greek writer Aristotle said a plot needed. In the 1800s, a German writer named Gustav Freytag developed this concept even more and divided plots into additional sections. His idea of plot structure is often called Freytag's Pyramid.

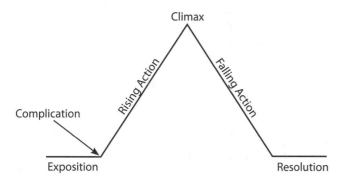

In Freytag's Pyramid, plots have exposition, complication, rising action, climax, falling action, and resolution. We are going to study each of these one at a time.

Exposition is easy to understand. It is when the writer introduces background information to help the reader understand the setting, characters, or events of the story a little better. Most of the time this happens near the beginning of a story. Here is a classic example from *Little House on the Prairie*, by Laura Ingalls Wilder.

> A long time ago, when all the grandfathers and grandmothers of today were little boys and little girls or very small babies, or perhaps not even born, Pa and Ma and Laura and Baby Carrie left their little house in the Big Woods of Wisconsin. They drove away and left it lonely and empty in the clearing among the big trees, and they never saw that little house again. They were going to Indian country.

In this example the reader is introduced to the setting, the main characters, and the context for what is going to come next.

Discussion Questions

Think about one of your favorite stories. Does it provide exposition at the beginning? What kinds of information does the exposition give you? Does the exposition appear later?

Objectives:

❶ Learn about exposition in plots.

❷ Read the assigned Bible passage.

❸ Answer questions about the assigned Bible passage.

❹ Write a paragraph.

❺ Read and discuss the assigned book (teacher's choice).

HINT! ⊰ The word *exposition* simply means to explain something.

Read and discuss assigned passage

Read the following Bible passage: Judges 6:1–27

Step One: Who is this passage about, and what is the cultural and historical setting?

_____

_____

_____

Step Two: What is the genre of this passage (history, poetry, prophecy, proverbs, letters, parables, etc.)?

_____

_____

_____

Step Three: What is the intended meaning of this passage? Some questions you can ask to help with this question are "What fallen or sinful condition is being highlighted in this passage?" or "What prompted the author to write this passage?" (Is this message about sin, salvation, faith, hope, etc.?)

_____

_____

_____

Step Four: Can you list other Bible passages that help define the intended meaning? (A concordance would be helpful here.)

_____

_____

_____

Step Five: Once the original meaning is understood, seek to find a simple life application.

_____

_____

_____

Read and discuss with your teacher

Answer the following questions about the passage:

1. What is the plot of this story (what are the events that happen)?

_____

_____

_____

2. Does the story have a recognizable beginning, middle, and end? How do you know?

_____

_____

_____

3. How does the plot connect with the story's theme? If you are not sure of what the story's theme is, think about the story's message. Does the plot connect to the message in some way?

_____

_____

_____

Complete the following activity

In the Bible passage you read this week, which part do you think is the exposition? Write a paragraph that explains which part is exposition. Be sure to indicate why that exposition was included. Use specific examples and be sure to start your paragraph with a topic sentence. Your sentences will need to flow well together.

_____

_____

_____

_____

_____

_____

_____

_____

_____

_____

_____

_____

_____

_____

_____

_____

_____

_____

Read and discuss assigned book

Remember to keep in mind these five principles when reading the book of your choice this week:

Step One: Determine the genre of the literature (historical fiction, fantasy, drama, Western, mystery, science fiction, poetry, biography, etc.).

_____

_____

_____

Step Two: Read the book, keeping in mind the main setting of the text and the primary roles of each character.

_____

_____

_____

Step Three: Look for the flow of the story. Describe the flow of the story from your book.

_____

_____

_____

Step Four: What is the book's message or what do you think it is trying to teach you?

_____

_____

_____

CONTINUED ON NEXT PAGE➔

Step Five: Does this message agree with what the Bible teaches? Why or why not?

_____

_____

_____

In the last lesson you learned that the point of view of the narrator tells you who is telling the story. Is the narrator a character in the story? If so, that story is written in first person. If the narrator is not a character in the story, it is written in third person. The second person voice is most often used in writing speeches, songs, and instructions. It is rarely used in literature, but when it is it makes the reader part of the story. It sounds like this:

> You sat at the counter and ordered a triple chocolate malted milkshake. You slurped and slurped until it was deliciously all gone. Then you burped.

A writer must be careful not to mix up the narrative voices in one story, although it's easy to do when you first start writing. It takes practice to remember to control the use of person.

Take a few minutes to review what you have learned about the narrative voice, then see if you can tell which voice the following statements are written in:

_____Lucy was nervous because this was her first time going to church camp. She was the last one to be picked up and hoped there would be enough room on the van for her. She placed her backpack in the cargo hold and got on, feeling a huge sense of relief when she saw that her best friend Gretchen had saved her a seat.

_____Please be patient as you wait for the church van to pick you up. Once it arrives please place your backpack in the cargo hold before finding your seat. You are going to have so much fun at Kamp Katchafish!

_____When the church van arrived, I placed my backpack in the cargo hold and got on. We were heading to church camp, and I was nervous. I relaxed, though, when I saw my best friend Gretchen sitting in the third row.

Objectives:

❶ Understand the different narrative voices.

❷ Control the use of person in your writing.

Writing

Today you will practice using third person by writing a paragraph of directions written in third person, using he, she, or they. This will be hard because you will want to use second person. You are going to describe how to do something. It will be easier if you tell how to do something simple.

A good way to start is to make a list of steps or procedures. They should be listed in the order in which they should be done. There should be at least eight steps in your list. You do not need to use complete sentences in your list. Read my example and then think of something you can write about.

How to Sharpen a Pencil

1. Face sharpener

2. Hold pencil in left hand, the end to be sharpened pointed to the right

3. Grasp handle on the right side of the sharpener with thumb and forefinger

4. Insert end of pencil in hole in top of the left end of sharpener

5. Turn crank clockwise facing right end of sharpener

6. Push on pencil while turning crank

7. Remove pencil and examine for sharpness (Repeat steps 4, 5, and 6 if necessary.)

8. Blow dust off sharpened end

Our next step is to turn our list into sentences in which the narrative voice uses **third person**. To make this example a paragraph, we will have to write a topic sentence. The following sentence should work as a topic sentence. If we put this sentence before the directions, we will have a fully developed paragraph.

Sharpening a pencil is an easy thing for a person to do.

CONTINUED ON NEXT PAGE ➔

I have made bold the use of third person in this example:

How to Sharpen a Pencil

Sharpening a pencil is an easy thing for a **person** to do. A **boy** who would like to do this faces the sharpener. **He** then holds **his** pencil in **his** left hand so that the end to be sharpened points to **his** right. Using **his** right hand, **he** holds the handle on the right side of the sharpener with **his** thumb and forefinger. With **his** left hand he inserts the end of **his** pencil in the hole in the top of the left end of the sharpener.

He turns the crank in a clockwise direction as **he** faces the right end of the sharpener and at the same time pushes the pencil into the sharpener. After a few turns of the handle, **he** removes **his** pencil and checks for sharpness. If it is not sharp enough, **he** repeats steps four, five, and six. When the pencil is sharp, **he** blows the dust off the end that has been sharpened.

Now it is your turn. You are to write a description in third person, just as we wrote how to sharpen a pencil in third person. (Do not write about how to sharpen a pencil.) You may use the sidebar of this page to write a list.

_____

_____

_____

_____

_____

_____

_____

_____

_____

_____

_____

Today you are to write the <u>same directions</u> that you wrote in the last two days, but this time they should be in **second person**, using *you*. This is the voice with which the writer talks directly to the reader and calls the reader *you*. This should sound like this:

> **You** are holding the pencil in **your** left hand, pointing the end to be sharpened to **your** right.

Notice that the narrative voice in this example speaks in present tense. You might want to try this in your paragraph.

_____

_____

_____

_____

_____

_____

_____

_____

_____

_____

_____

Previously, you wrote directions in **third person**, using *he*, then the same directions in **second person**, using *you*. Today you will write the same directions in **first person**, using *I*. This is the choice in which the narrative voice talks about itself. This should sound like this:

    I hold the pencil in **my** left hand with the end to be sharpened pointing to **my** right.

_____

_____

_____

_____

_____

_____

_____

_____

_____

_____

_____

_____

In this exercise, you should have learned to control use of the person of your narrative voice. Explain these three voices to your teacher, explaining how you used them in each of your paragraphs.

Fill out the "Student Progress Report" on the next page.

Remember to fill out the writing skills mastery check-off form and, if necessary, to record spelling words and other problems that you need to address in the future.

Student Progress Report

This is the best sentence I wrote this week:

_____

_____

_____

_____

I think it is the best because:

_____

_____

_____

_____

I made this mistake this week and this is what I learned to help me avoid making the mistake again:

_____

_____

_____

_____

This is the sentence showing how I fixed the mistake:

_____

_____

_____

_____

Comments:

_____

_____

_____

_____

Your teacher will assign a book for you to read this week. Be sure to finish it before the end of the week. Review the five steps of reading literature and prepare to describe each of the five elements from your book.

Name of the book: _____

Author of the book: _____

Read and discuss with your teacher

We have learned that plots usually start with some exposition that gives the reader background on the story, including information on the main characters, the setting, and what is going on.

This week we will study the **complication** element. For a plot to be a story, there needs to be a sequence of events for readers to follow. Your character must want or need something and set out to get/achieve it. The complication is something that could stand in the way of their success.

The complication can be many things — an illness, bad weather, conflict between characters, etc. — but what makes it the complication is that it leads to the rest of the plot. If something bad happens, but it is not related to the main character's goal, then that is not the complication. The complication also needs to occur early in the story since it sets up the action that follows. Not every difficulty the characters encounter is the complication — it needs to be what throws the whole story into motion for it to be the complication. Let's discover what the complication is in *Anne of Green Gables*, by L.M. Montgomery.

> Anne Shirley is a young orphan who longs to be adopted into a loving family. Siblings Matthew and Marilla Cuthbert decide to adopt a young boy because Matthew is getting too old to do all the farm chores by himself. When Matthew goes to the train station to pick up the boy, he discovers the orphanage has made a mistake and sent a girl (Anne) instead. Anne is crushed to discover she was not the child they wanted. Matthew wants to keep her, but Marilla wants to take her back to the orphanage. Marilla eventually gives in, but often wonders if they made the right decision because Anne has a way of complicating their lives instead of making it easier. The story covers several years of Anne's life — full of one amusing adventure after another — as Anne wins the hearts of Matthew and Marilla. Just as she is preparing to move away for college, Matthew has a heart attack and dies upon learning that the bank where they have all their money has failed, and they are now destitute. Anne had worked

Objectives:

❶ Learn about complication in plots.

❷ Read the assigned Bible passage.

❸ Answer questions about the assigned Bible passage.

❹ Write a paragraph.

❺ Read and discuss the assigned book (teacher's choice).

HINT! ⸞ A complication is simply a circumstance that complicates something.

CONTINUED ON NEXT PAGE →

hard to earn a scholarship for college but chooses to stay in Avonlea and get a job in order to help Marilla save the farm.

In this story, the complication is that Anne is a girl and not a boy. This is what sets the story in motion, as Matthew and Marilla have to make a decision about keeping her or sending her back.

Discussion Questions

Think about one of your favorite stories. What is the complication in the plot? How do you know that it is the complication?

Read and discuss assigned passage

Read the following Bible passage: Ruth 1:1–22

Step One: Who is this passage about, and what is the cultural and historical setting?

_____

_____

_____

Step Two: What is the genre of this passage (history, poetry, prophecy, proverbs, letters, parables, etc.)?

_____

_____

_____

Step Three: What is the intended meaning of this passage? Some questions you can ask to help with this question are "What fallen or sinful condition is being highlighted in this passage?" or "What prompted the author to write this passage?" (Is this message about sin, salvation, faith, hope, etc.?)

_____

_____

_____

Step Four: Can you list other Bible passages that help define the intended meaning? (A concordance would be helpful here.)

_____

_____

_____

Step Five: Once the original meaning is understood, seek to find a simple life application.

_____

_____

_____

Read and discuss with your teacher

Answer the following questions about the passage:

1. What is the plot of this story (what are the events that happen)?

_____

_____

_____

2. Does the story have a recognizable beginning, middle, and end? How do you know?

_____

_____

_____

3. How does the plot connect with the story's theme? If you are not sure of what the story's theme is, think about the story's message. Does the plot connect to the message in some way?

_____

_____

_____

Complete the following activity

Write a paragraph describing the complication in this week's Bible passage. Be sure to include a topic sentence and explain your reasoning.

_____

_____

_____

_____

_____

_____

_____

_____

_____

_____

_____

_____

_____

_____

_____

_____

_____

_____

Read and discuss assigned book

Remember to keep in mind these five principles when reading the book of your choice this week:

Step One: Determine the genre of the literature (historical fiction, fantasy, drama, Western, mystery, science fiction, poetry, biography, etc.).

_____

_____

_____

Step Two: Read the book, keeping in mind the main setting of the text and the primary roles of each character.

_____

_____

_____

Step Three: Look for the flow of the story. Describe the flow of the story from your book.

_____

_____

_____

Step Four: What is the book's message or what do you think it is trying to teach you?

_____

_____

_____

CONTINUED ON NEXT PAGE→

Step Five: Does this message agree with what the Bible teaches? Why or why not?

_____

_____

_____

Most stories are written in past tense, but there are a very few that are written in present tense. In this exercise, you will have a chance to change the tense of a story from **past tense to present tense**.

Past tense talks about things that have already happened.

> Bill **saw** the dog.

Present tense talks about things that are happening at the time of the reading.

> Bill **sees** the dog. Bill is **seeing** the dog.

The following examples will show you how this is done.

PAST TENSE: When Mary <u>put</u> her shoes on after swimming, she <u>felt</u> the frog that Bill <u>had put there</u> when nobody <u>was</u> looking.

PRESENT TENSE: When Mary <u>puts</u> her shoes on after swimming, she <u>feels</u> the frog Bill <u>has put there</u> when nobody was looking.

Explain to your teacher how to write in the past tense and also the present tense.

Objectives:

❶ Understand how past tense works.

❷ Understand how a change from past to present tense in a story changes the story.

❸ Change past tense to present tense in a story.

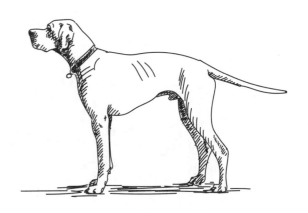

Pick out any chapter book of fiction that your teacher agrees for you to use. This narrative should be written in **past tense**. Show your teacher the clues that tell you the book is written in past tense. The first words on the first page and first line on the next page and the first few lines on the last page will tell you if this writer is consistent in the use of tenses. Write these lines out and evaluate them. Does the author use past tense in all the sentences you wrote down?

_____

_____

_____

_____

_____

_____

_____

_____

_____

_____

_____

_____

_____

_____

_____

_____

_____

_____

_____

Writing

Turn part of the story you picked out into present tense. It will be like you and the writer are working together on the story, and you are going to rewrite a section. Pick two pages of the story to **change the tense to present tense**. Today you will rewrite the first page of the story on the Story Worksheet 1.

1. **Your name** (first and last) and the **date** should be in the upper right hand corner.

2. There should be a **title on the first line** — no quote marks or underlining, and there should be capitals.

3. **Skip** the second line and **start** your paper about your two-page rewriting on the **third line** of the paper.

4. You should start by **identifying the pages** (by number) you have rewritten.

5. Give the **name of the story**.

6. Identify who has rewritten the two pages of it (your name).

7. Skip a line and start the rewriting.

Your Name

The Date

SPACE

SPACE

Your Title

SPACE

Pages ___ and ___ of ___Name of Story___ rewritten by

Your name _____

Your two pages of the story rewritten

Story Worksheet

_____

_____

_____

_____

_____

_____

_____

_____

_____

_____

_____

_____

_____

_____

_____

_____

_____

_____

_____

_____

_____

_____

_____

_____

_____

_____

_____

_____

_____

_____

Today you will rewrite the second page of the story from your book on the Story Worksheet 2.

_____

_____

_____

_____

_____

_____

_____

_____

_____

_____

_____

_____

_____

_____

_____

_____

_____

_____

_____

_____

_____

_____

_____

Read what you have written to someone else before you give it to your teacher. You might start reading a page or two before the place where you have rewritten it, and, when you are done reading, you might ask your listener what there was about the story that was strange or out of place. This is to see if the shifting of tenses is noticed by your listener.

Fill out the "Student Progress Report" on the next page.

Remember to fill out the writing skills mastery check-off form and, if necessary, to record spelling words and other problems that you need to address in the future.

CONTINUED ON NEXT PAGE ➜

Student Progress Report

This is the best sentence I wrote this week:

_____

_____

_____

_____

I think it is the best because:

_____

_____

_____

_____

I made this mistake this week, and this is what I learned to help me avoid making the mistake again:

_____

_____

_____

_____

This is the sentence showing how I fixed this mistake:

_____

_____

_____

_____

Comments:

_____

_____

_____

_____

Your teacher will assign a book for you to read this week. Be sure to finish it before the end of the week. Review the five steps of reading literature and prepare to describe each of the five elements from your book.

Name of the book: _____

Author of the book: _____

Read and discuss with your teacher

We have learned that plots have exposition to introduce the setting, characters, and situation. Then they have a complication, which sets the actual story into motion. After the complication is the **rising action** of the plot.

The rising action is a series of events that follow the complication and build excitement until the climax or turning point in the story. The main character or characters will want something or will want to do something (problem). If the character gets what he or she wants right away the story will be boring, and this is where the rising action comes in. In most stories, there will be forces that will try to keep the main characters from getting what they want. These may be natural forces like gravity or winter weather. They may be other people like teachers or neighbors or cruel neighborhood bullies. Let's look at an example from *Charlotte's Web*, by E.B. White.

> Wilbur, a newborn pig and runt of the litter, is rescued from an early death by the owner's daughter, Fern. Fern makes a pet of Wilbur and loves him dearly. When he grows too large for their home, Fern's father takes him to live on a nearby farm. Wilbur eventually makes friends with the other barnyard animals; his closest friend being a spider named Charlotte. He soon learns that his new owner, Mr. Zuckerman, intends to fatten him up in order to turn him into ham and bacon, and once again, Wilbur's life is in danger. Like Fern, Charlotte saves Wilbur from certain death by making a plea for his worth to Mr. Zuckerman. She does this by weaving a series of spider webs that spell out words that compliment Wilbur. Wilbur becomes famous as the webs become the talk of the town. Mr. Zuckerman is still planning to kill Wilbur in the fall, but he decides to show him at the county fair first. Wilbur and Charlotte realize that he must win "Best Pig" at the fair in order to have a shot at living a long life.

Objectives:

❶ Learn about rising action in plots.

❷ Read the assigned Bible passage.

❸ Answer questions about the assigned Bible passage.

❹ Write a paragraph.

❺ Read and discuss the assigned book (teacher's choice).

HINT! ⸙ Rising action consists of developments and difficulties that occur and are related to the problem. It adds suspense and builds reader interest in the story.

CONTINUED ON NEXT PAGE ➜

The main problem in this story is Wilbur's impending death. Initially it appears he has been rescued by Fern, but the complication occurs when Fern's father gives Wilbur to a neighboring farmer who intends to fatten him up for meat. How will he escape his fate now? The **rising action** is the series of events that occur because of the word webs created by Charlotte, that eventually convince Mr. Zuckerman to show Wilbur at the county fair. What happens at the fair is the climax of the story — will Mr. Zuckerman change his mind? The rising action always leads to the climax.

Discussion Question

Think about one of your favorite stories. What is the rising action in the plot? How do you know that it is rising action and not the complication?

Read and discuss assigned passage

Read the following Bible passage: 1 Samuel 16:1–13

Step One: Who is this passage about, and what is the cultural and historical setting?

_____

_____

_____

Step Two: What is the genre of this passage (history, poetry, prophecy, proverbs, letters, parables, etc.)?

_____

_____

_____

Step Three: What is the intended meaning of this passage? Some questions you can ask to help with this question are "What fallen or sinful condition is being highlighted in this passage?" or "What prompted the author to write this passage?" (Is this message about sin, salvation, faith, hope, etc.?)

_____

_____

_____

Step Four: Can you list other Bible passages that help define the intended meaning? (A concordance would be helpful here.)

_____

_____

_____

Step Five: Once the original meaning is understood, seek to find a simple life application.

_____

_____

_____

Read and discuss with your teacher

Answer the following questions about the passage:

1. What is the plot of this story (what are the events that happen)?

_____

_____

_____

2. Does the story have a recognizable beginning, middle, and end? How do you know?

_____

_____

_____

3. How does the plot connect with the story's theme? If you are not sure of what the story's theme is, think about the story's message. Does the plot connect to the message in some way?

_____

_____

_____

Complete the following activity

Identify the rising action in this week's passage. Write a paragraph explaining how you know it is the rising action. Be sure to use specific examples and to explain your thinking. Include a topic sentence at the beginning of your paragraph.

_____

_____

_____

_____

_____

_____

_____

_____

_____

_____

_____

_____

_____

_____

_____

_____

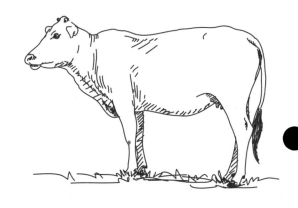

Read and discuss assigned book

Remember to keep in mind these five principles when reading the book of your choice this week:

Step One: Determine the genre of the literature (historical fiction, fantasy, drama, Western, mystery, science fiction, poetry, biography, etc.).

_____

_____

_____

Step Two: Read the book, keeping in mind the main setting of the text and the primary roles of each character.

_____

_____

_____

Step Three: Look for the flow of the story. Describe the flow of the story from your book.

_____

_____

_____

Step Four: What is the book's message or what do you think it is trying to teach you?

_____

_____

_____

CONTINUED ON NEXT PAGE➔

Step Five: Does this message agree with what the Bible teaches? Why or why not?

_____

_____

_____

Prewriting

To show how tenses work, I will use a story as an example that everyone is familiar with and has a character we all know. The wolf in the "Three Little Pigs" is not very bright. In fact, he tries to get at the pigs by blowing on their houses, which is not smart at all.

In most versions of this story, the narrative voice does not show the wolf thinking at all. But that wolf must have some idea about what is going on. It is important to know that a character's thoughts should be consistent with what you know about that character.

Characters and people think in all tenses. This is what it looks like when the wolf thinks in **past tense**:

> "Those are the three little houses that I saw the pigs build yesterday. Maybe they built houses that were not strong."

This is what it looks like when a character thinks in **present tense**:

> "This house appears to be made of straw, and I am standing out here and that pig is sitting in there, and we are both thinking about dinner!"

This is what it looks like when a character thinks in **future tense**:

> "In just a little while I will blow this house down. I will have to keep my eyes peeled for that little porker. When the house goes, my dinner will be running for safety."

Objectives:

❶ Learn and practice the use of past, present, and future tenses.

Writing

You will practice writing the wolf's thoughts in different tenses. I will give you a writing prompt to help you think about what the wolf might be thinking, and you will write some thoughts the wolf might have. Be sure to keep the tense of the wolf's thoughts consistent in each exercise.

1. Write some of the wolf's thoughts in **past tense**.

    As the walls of the straw house began to lean away from the wolf, and the roof began to lift, the wolf thought,

    _____

    _____

    _____

    _____

2. Write some of the wolf's thoughts in **present tense**:

    The wolf's hay fever gets the best of him and he begins to sneeze just as the house begins to fall. He has to hold his nose to keep the straw dust out of it. He thinks,

    _____

    _____

    _____

    _____

3. Add to the wolf's thoughts in **future tense**:

    "When this straw house finally falls and the dust clears, I am going to have a lovely dinner. The first thing I will do is . . .

    _____

    _____

    _____

    _____

Present tense is used to describe actions that are taking place at the time of the telling of the event.
    Example: *John is in the house. Mr. Jones lives there.*
Past tense is used to describe actions that have already happened.
    Example: *John was in the house. Mr. Jones lived there.*
Future tense is used to describe actions that will happen.
    Example: *John will be in the house. Mr. Jones will live there.*

You are to make up thoughts for a character.

Ask your teacher to select a short story for you. It should be written in past tense. You are to work with a number of pages in it from a point selected by your teacher. Even if the author has the main character thinking in the story your teacher selects for you, add to the thoughts the main character has.

Remember, the character's thoughts should be consistent with what you know about that character. If you recognize that character to be kind and gentle, then that character's thoughts should be kind and gentle.

In the next three days of lessons, you will finish the story your teacher chose for you from the spot your teacher selected. Make sure your character thinks in all three tenses.

Start your story on the Past, Present, and Future Worksheet using the chart as an example. Today write part of the story in past tense.

Your Name

The Date

SPACE

SPACE

Your Title

SPACE

Story title

Character's name

Pages used

Character's thoughts in past tense:

Character's thoughts in present tense:

Character's thoughts in future tense:

CONTINUED ON NEXT PAGE➔

Today you will write the character's thoughts in present tense. You can practice in the space below but write your final version on the Past, Present, and Future Worksheet.

_____

_____

_____

_____

_____

_____

_____

_____

_____

_____

_____

_____

_____

_____

_____

_____

_____

_____

_____

_____

_____

_____

_____

_____

_____

Today you will write the character's thoughts in future tense. You can practice in the space below but write your final version on the Past, Present, and Future Worksheet.

_____

_____

_____

_____

_____

_____

_____

_____

_____

_____

_____

_____

_____

_____

_____

_____

_____

_____

Fill out the "Student Progress Report" on the next page.

Remember to fill out the writing skills mastery check-off form and, if necessary, to record spelling words and other problems that you need to address in the future.

 **Writing Lesson 9**

Student Progress Report

This is the best sentence I wrote this week:

_____

_____

_____

_____

I think it is the best because:

_____

_____

_____

_____

I made this mistake this week and this is what I learned to help me avoid making the mistake again:

_____

_____

_____

_____

This is the sentence showing how I fixed the mistake:

_____

_____

_____

_____

Comments:

_____

_____

_____

_____

Your teacher will assign a book for you to read this week. Be sure to finish it before the end of the week. Review the five steps of reading literature and prepare to describe each of the five elements from your book.

Name of the book: _____

Author of the book: _____

Read and discuss with your teacher

We have learned about exposition, complication, and rising action in plots. These elements all help develop the story. Exposition provides the reader with background, complication starts the story, and rising action increases the tension and suspense in the story.

The greatest moment of tension is the climax. This is the turning point in the story. Things may be looking pretty bad for the hero of the story until the climax happens. If a story is about a difficult journey, the climax might be the last obstacle the characters face. If the story is about a conflict between a good guy and the bad guy, the climax might be a showdown between them.

In *The Bronze Bow*, by Elizabeth George Speare, the main character is eighteen-year-old Daniel, a Galilean who is filled with hatred toward the Romans because they executed his father. Daniel nurses his bitterness by joining in on the brutal raids of a band of outlaws. The more he plots against the Romans, the more his hatred grows, until he is almost destroyed by it. When he begins hearing stories of a man named Jesus, his bitterness is challenged. The **climax** comes when he meets Jesus face to face. Jesus teaches about a new kingdom where the tools of battle are love, humility, and sacrifice and that Daniel must "make ready his heart and mind" to enter this kingdom. Daniel eventually chooses to trust Jesus and is finally set free from his hatred.

A climax can be about many things, but it is always the most exciting part of the story. It is not usually the end of the story, but it is the turning point that sets the ending in motion, just as how the complication sets the plot itself in motion.

Discussion Questions

Think of one of your favorite stories. What is the climax of the plot? How do you know it is the climax and not another part of the plot?

Objectives:

❶ Learn about climax in plots.

❷ Read the assigned Bible passage.

❸ Answer questions about the assigned Bible passage.

❹ Write a paragraph.

❺ Read and discuss the assigned book (teacher's choice).

HINT! ∉ The climax will always be the most exciting part of a story.

Read and discuss assigned passage

Read the following Bible passage: Esther 3:1–14, 4:10–5:14, 7:1–10

Step One: Who is this passage about, and what is the cultural and historical setting?

_____

_____

_____

Step Two: What is the genre of this passage (history, poetry, prophecy, proverbs, letters, parables, etc.)?

_____

_____

_____

Step Three: What is the intended meaning of this passage? Some questions you can ask to help with this question are "What fallen or sinful condition is being highlighted in this passage?" or "What prompted the author to write this passage?" (Is this message about sin, salvation, faith, hope, etc.?)

_____

_____

_____

Step Four: Can you list other Bible passages that help define the intended meaning? (A concordance would be helpful here.)

_____

_____

_____

Step Five: Once the original meaning is understood, seek to find a simple life application.

_____

_____

_____

Read and discuss with your teacher

Answer the following questions about the passage:

1. What is the plot of this story (what are the events that happen)?

_____

_____

_____

2. Does the story have a recognizable beginning, middle, and end? How do you know?

_____

_____

_____

3. How does the plot connect with the story's theme? If you are not sure of what the story's theme is, think about the story's message. Does the plot connect to the message in some way?

_____

_____

_____

Complete the following activity

Identify the plot climax in this week's Bible passage. Write a paragraph explaining what it is and explaining why that is the plot climax.

_____

_____

_____

_____

_____

_____

_____

_____

_____

_____

_____

_____

_____

_____

_____

_____

Read and discuss assigned book

Remember to keep in mind these five principles when reading the book of your choice this week:

Step One: Determine the genre of the literature (historical fiction, fantasy, drama, Western, mystery, science fiction, poetry, biography, etc.)

_____

_____

_____

Step Two: Read the book, keeping in mind the main setting of the text and the primary roles of each character.

_____

_____

_____

Step Three: Look for the flow of the story. Describe the flow of the story from your book.

_____

_____

_____

Step Four: What is the book's message or what do you think it is trying to teach you?

_____

_____

_____

Step Five: Does this message agree with what the Bible teaches? Why or why not?

_____

_____

_____

CONTINUED ON NEXT PAGE ➔

Problems I Have Solved This First Semester

1. _____

   _____

2. _____

   _____

3. _____

   _____

4. _____

   _____

5. _____

   _____

6. _____

   _____

7. _____

   _____

8. _____

   _____

How I feel about this progress I am making:

_____

_____

> **"**
>
> For we are not writing any
> other things to you than
> what you read or understand...
> Paul (2 Corinthians 1:13)

Prewriting

There is much more to being an adult than just growing older. Thinking clearly and presenting ideas well to others is another way of being grown up. The more experience people have with using their language, the better they get at it.

An important way to learn to use language effectively is to write it. It takes practice to be good at anything, and it will take practice using your language to be able to use it as well as your teacher or older friends do.

One difference between the way students use language and the way adults use it, is that many adults organize what they say. This is especially true when they write. It is an important skill to be able to communicate written information in an organized way.

A good place to start is with a paragraph. There are six steps to writing an organized paragraph. This exercise will give you practice in all six.

STEP ONE: Break the subject into parts.

You must be able to break into parts any subject you want to write a paragraph about.

Let's pretend we have been assigned to write a paper about a student's doll. Upon breaking the idea of a doll into its parts, we would find that it has different kinds of parts. Some of them would be physical parts, and some of them would be non-physical.

First, let's look at the physical parts of a doll. There are:

1. Two arms
   a. Two elbows
   b. Two hands
2. Two legs
   a. Two knees
   b. Two feet

3. One head
   a. Two eyes
   b. One nose
   c. One mouth
   d. Hair
   e. Two ears

4. One body
   a. Chest
   b. Torso
   c. Hips — and so on

Objectives:

❶ Organize a group of ideas.

❷ Write a sentence that introduces a group of ideas.

❸ Construct a paragraph based on a group of ideas.

CONTINUED ON NEXT PAGE➔

Now look at the non-physical parts of a doll. The idea of dolls can be broken into their:

1. Types

    a. Baby doll

    b. Display doll (The kind adults collect and display on shelves.)

    c. Paper doll

    d. Realistic doll

2. Function

    a. Dependent (baby needs a mother)

    b. Independent (grown up looking)

We now have a list of the parts of a doll. The list could be physical parts or non-physical parts. We really have enough parts here for lots of paragraphs. We could use just the first list to make our paragraph. This list has four parts:

1. Arms   2. Legs

3. Head   4. Body

Using this list, our paragraph would have at least four sentences in it.

HINT! When you organize your material, you organize your reader's mind.

STEP TWO: Organize the list.

We have to decide in what order we want the sentences. There are a number of ways to order (organize) the items in a paragraph. Some of these ways are:

1. By **size**

2. By **beauty** — the most beautiful first, the second most beautiful next and so on

3. By **importance**

4. By **cost**

5. By **time** — what happened first, what happened next and so on

6. By what you **like** most first, and what you like second next and so on

7. By **top to bottom** or **right to left**

Let's use number seven, top to bottom. That makes sense when talking about a doll. The order of the parts of our paragraph about the doll is:

1. Head

2. Body

3. Arms

4. Legs

This will give us the order and the structure of our paragraph. Let's start with point number one, the head. We have to decide if we can tell our readers all they need to know about our doll's head in just a few sentences. Look at the items under head — there are five things we would have to talk about. We might have to use five sentences just about the head.

CONTINUED ON NEXT PAGE→

STEP THREE: Narrow the topic. (Write about just a small part of the original topic.)

Let's not write our paragraph about the doll just yet. The subject is too big. Let's write a paragraph about just the head of the doll.
We must put in order the parts of the head. Let's start at the top and work down again. This means we have to make another list of the parts of the head.

1. Hair

2. Eyes

3. Ears

4. Mouth

We have the order, the structure, and enough material for a paragraph on the head.

STEP FOUR: Turn items into sentences.

We must write at least one sentence about each item of the head. Let's do that now.

1. Hair: The hair is long and silky and has a slight curl in it.

2. Eyes: When the doll is turned on its back, the large, blue eyes close.

3. Ears: I know my doll cannot hear me with its tiny ears, but I like to tell it secrets that I never would tell a real, living person.

4. Mouth: There is always a smile on the lips.

STEP FIVE: Write a topic sentence.

Once we have the body of our paragraph, we need a topic sentence. A topic sentence introduces our reader to the information in the paragraph, but it also limits what we can talk about in the paragraph. If the topic sentence tells our reader that the doll costs a lot of money, then we cannot talk about how beautiful the doll is. We would have to talk about the cost of the doll.

Since we are writing about the head of the doll today, our topic sentence must introduce the head. Here is an example of a topic sentence.

"The part of my doll I like best is the head."

STEP SIX: Put it all together.

We now have the whole paragraph about the head of the doll. I have numbered the parts of this example paragraph so you could see where those parts came from in the listing in **step four**.

(TS) The part of my doll I like best is the head. **(1)** The hair is long and silky and has a slight curl in it. **(2)** When the doll is turned on its back, the large, blue eyes close. **(3)** I know my doll cannot hear me with its tiny ears, but I like to tell it secrets that I never would tell a real, living person. **(4)** No matter what I say, there is always a smile on its lips.

HINT! A well-constructed paragraph can be a joy to read.

Writing

In the first three days you did not have to write anything, but you know that will change, right? You have learned that there are six steps to writing an organized paragraph. They are:

1. **Break the subject** into parts.

2. Put the parts into some **order**.

3. **Narrow** the topic.

4. Write **sentences** for the parts.

5. Write the **topic sentence**.

6. **Put it all together**.

If you have understood this, you are learning to think in an organized and adult way.

To write an organized paragraph, you have to pick a topic. This is not a problem. I will give you some suggestions:

1. My dog or cat

2. A new tool

3. My best friend

4. My room

5. The game I like to play best

6. The food I would rather not eat

7. My new bike (game, ball, pet, or friend)

You are to use our six steps to write this paragraph. (Do not to write about a doll.)

STEP ONE: Break the subject into parts.

Write the subject of your paragraph: _____

Write the parts this subject can be broken into. They can be physical or non-physical.

1. _____

2. _____

CONTINUED ON NEXT PAGE ➔

3. _____

4. _____

You do not have to use four parts, there can be three or five or eight. If you have more, write them in the sidebar of this page. It depends on the subject and how you want to break it down.

STEP TWO: List the parts in order. Remember, you have a choice here.

Write the method you will use to organize the parts: (top to bottom, small to big and so on) _____

List again the parts, but in the order you will write about them:

1. _____

2. _____

3. _____

4. _____

STEP THREE: Narrow your topic.

Look at your list and choose one item to write a paragraph about. Write your new topic here:_____

Now make a new list of parts for the item you chose.

1. _____

2. _____

3. _____

STEP FOUR: Make sentences out of the steps in the list.

1. _____

2. _____

3. _____

STEP FIVE: Write the topic sentence. (Remember that it has to introduce what will be in the paragraph and it will also limit what you can put in the paragraph to the subject of the topic sentence.)

_____

_____

_____

STEP SIX: Write your paper (paragraph) on the Paragraph Worksheet. Just before you hand it to your teacher, check it against the example to be sure all the parts are where they should be.

You could title this paper "One Good Paragraph" and, with pride, show it to your teacher.

HINT! Go back and turn two of your sentences that are connected by subject into either a compound or a complex sentence. See Lesson 1.

Your Name
The Date

SPACE

SPACE

Your Title

SPACE

Topic Sentence indented

The body of your paragraph

CONTINUED ON NEXT PAGE ➔

_____

_____

_____

_____

_____

_____

_____

_____

_____

_____

_____

_____

_____

_____

_____

_____

_____

_____

_____

_____

_____

_____

_____

_____

_____

Fill out the "Student Progress Report" on the next page.

Remember to fill out the writing skills mastery check-off form and, if necessary, to record spelling words and other problems that you need to address in the future.

Student Progress Report

This is the best sentence I wrote this week:

_____

_____

_____

_____

I think it is the best because:

_____

_____

_____

_____

I made this mistake this week, and this is what I learned to help me avoid making the mistake again:

_____

_____

_____

_____

This is the sentence showing how I fixed this mistake:

_____

_____

_____

_____

Comments:

_____

_____

_____

_____

Your teacher will assign a book for you to read this week. Be sure to finish it before the end of the week. Review the five steps of reading literature and prepare to describe each of the five elements from your book.

Name of the book: _____

Author of the book: _____

Read and discuss with your teacher

We have learned about several elements of plot the past few weeks. Exposition introduces the setting, characters, and situation. The complication puts the plot in motion, and the rising action adds tension and interest. The climax is the most exciting part of the story.

The falling action follows the climax. Things are still happening, but now things are moving toward the end and storylines are being tied up. The climax has already determined how the story will end, though the reader may not yet understand what the ending is. The falling action pushes the plot along to the ending that the climax scene has developed.

In *The Swiss Family Robinson*, by Johann David Wyss, you have the story of a family of six who leave their native Switzerland for hope of a new life in Australia. The ship they are sailing on is damaged in a storm and they find themselves stranded on a deserted island where they learn to not only survive, but thrive. The climax of the story is when one of the older sons discovers a teenage girl who is also stranded on the island and has been captured by a band of pirates. The family helps her escape and elude the pirates until she is rescued by her father, Colonel Montrose. The falling action is when Colonel Montrose offers the family passage to England on his ship, and they have to decide whether to go to England or stay on the island they now call home.

Discussion Question

Think about one of your favorite stories. What is the falling action part of the plot? How do you know that it is falling action?

Objectives:

❶ Learn about falling action in plots.

❷ Read the assigned Bible passage.

❸ Answer questions about the assigned Bible passage.

❹ Write a paragraph.

❺ Read and discuss an assigned book (teacher's choice).

HINT! "Tension" refers to the reader's anticipation of more problems to come for the main character(s).

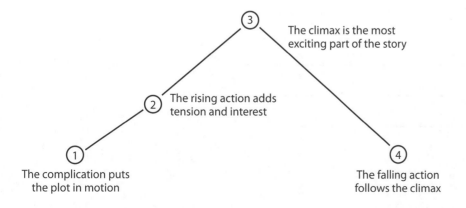

3 — The climax is the most exciting part of the story

2 — The rising action adds tension and interest

1 — The complication puts the plot in motion

4 — The falling action follows the climax

Read and discuss assigned passage

Read the following Bible passage: Nehemiah 1:1–2:13

Step One: Who is this passage about, and what is the cultural and historical setting?

_____

_____

_____

Step Two: What is the genre of this passage (history, poetry, prophecy, proverbs, letters, parables, etc.)?

_____

_____

_____

Step Three: What is the intended meaning of this passage? Some questions you can ask to help with this question are "What fallen or sinful condition is being highlighted in this passage?" or "What prompted the author to write this passage?" (Is this message about sin, salvation, faith, hope, etc.?)

_____

_____

_____

Step Four: Can you list other Bible passages that help define the intended meaning? (A concordance would be helpful here.)

_____

_____

_____

Step Five: Once the original meaning is understood, seek to find a simple life application.

_____

_____

_____

Read and discuss with your teacher

Answer the following questions about the passage:

1. What is the plot of this story (what are the events that happen)?

_____

_____

_____

2. Does the story have a recognizable beginning, middle, and end? How do you know?

_____

_____

_____

3. How does the plot connect with the story's theme? If you are not sure of what the story's theme is, think about the story's message. Does the plot connect to the message in some way?

_____

_____

_____

4. What is the exposition? What is the complication? What is the rising action? What is the climax?

_____

_____

_____

Complete the following activity

Identify the falling action in the passage you read for this week. Write a well-organized paragraph explaining what the falling action is and why you know that part is the falling action and not another element of the plot.

_____

_____

_____

_____

_____

_____

_____

_____

_____

_____

_____

Read and discuss assigned book

Remember to keep in mind these five principles when reading the book of your choice this week:

Step One: Determine the genre of the literature (historical fiction, fantasy, drama, Western, mystery, science fiction, poetry, biography, etc.)

_____

_____

_____

Step Two: Read the book, keeping in mind the main setting of the text and the primary roles of each character.

_____

_____

_____

Step Three: Look for the flow of the story. Describe the flow of the story from your book.

_____

_____

_____

Step Four: What is the book's message or what do you think it is trying to teach you?

_____

_____

_____

CONTINUED ON NEXT PAGE→

Step Five: Does this message agree with what the Bible teaches? Why or why not?

_____

_____

_____

Prewriting

The three parts of the "My Home" exercise will teach you to write descriptions that are accurate. If you are careful with the work of the next few days, you should be able to do a good job writing descriptions.

In this part of the exercise, you are to make a floor plan (map) of your home. This means that when you are done, your floor plan will look like your home would look if some giant were to take off the roof and look straight down on it from high above, or if some bird were to look down on it. (That is where we get the term bird's-eye view.) Your floor plan might include a kitchen, living room, bedrooms, den, closets, and outside doors. Do not forget any bathroom or hallways.

When you draw a bird's-eye view of a room, some of the things in the room should not be drawn. For instance, the giant would not be able to see the clocks or the pictures. She would be looking straight down. She would be able to see the floors, the halls, and the spaces where the doors are. So that is all you should put in your floor plan.

How big the rooms are and how long and how wide the halls are is not important. It will not be necessary to measure them. It would be good to try to make the relationships reasonable, though. Your teacher may show you how to do this by pacing off a room in both directions. You will see that the room is square or that it is longer in one way than it is in the other. In either case, your floor plan should show the relationships of the lengths to the widths for the rooms and the halls.

Of course, a hallway would be longer than it is wide. You may want to pace off the hall with your teacher and ask to be shown on scrap paper the relationship of the length to the width of the area. While you are learning this, you might ask about the relationship of the size of your bedroom to the size of the hall outside your room. This will help you when you make your floor plan. Notice on the drawing of the hallway (below right) that it is three times as long as it is wide. This is how you can talk about relationships of sizes.

Objectives:

❶ Understand the layout of a building.

❷ Show relationships of spaces in floor plans.

❸ Use a bird's-eye view.

❹ Create a drawing from what you see.

Hallway

Sample floor plans

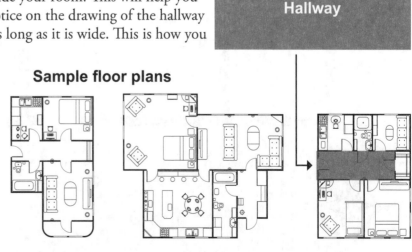

CONTINUED ON NEXT PAGE➔

Writing

After your teacher shows you how to figure relationships in size, take a trip through the house. Take the Floor Plan Worksheet and a pencil. You will need to make a rough sketch of where the doors and rooms are.

All maps and floor plans have north at the top of the page. If you are not sure about directions, have your teacher show you which direction is north. The north side of the house should be at the top of your paper. On maps the four cardinal directions are denoted with a compass rose, showing north, south, east, and west, as shown with the image below.

When making any map or writing descriptions, you should always start with general areas or statements first. So, the first things you should draw are the outside walls and the main rooms. (Remember you are looking down from high above your house.) This will let you see how the building is laid out. Your teacher may pace off the rooms with you, and when you get back to your work area, your teacher may show you how to figure how much larger some of the rooms are than others.

Today, complete your notes about the floor plan by pacing off the rooms, etc., and using the Floor Plan Worksheet for your notes. You might want to make notes about which part of your house is on the north side, and whether your house is a square or a rectangle or something else. If you pace off the rooms in your house, you will want to write that information down, too.

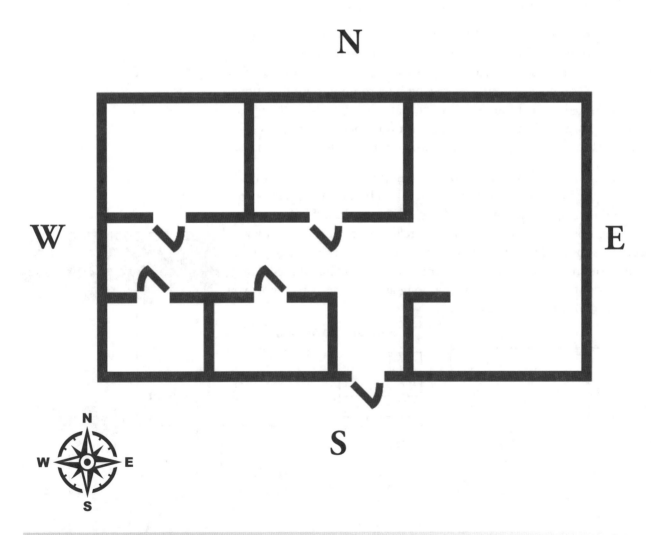

CONTINUED ON NEXT PAGE →

Floor Plan Worksheet

Notes:

_____

_____

_____

_____

_____

_____

_____

Students may use blank spaces to include any rough sketches in addition to the notes.

Today, complete a rough drawing of the outside walls and the positions of the outside doors. If you have trouble with this part, be sure to ask your teacher to help you because it will be hard for you to continue if this is not understood or done correctly. Remember to use your notes! It is okay if you have to erase and fix mistakes. You will have a chance to make a fresh, clean copy of your floor plan. The important thing is to make an accurate sketch. You may use empty spaces on this page for sketches.

Today, draw in the major room areas, which may include portions of your previous sketches. Be sure to fix any mistakes you may have made, and then add the rooms. Remember to use your notes! You will have a chance to make a fresh, clean copy of your floor plan. The important thing is to make an accurate sketch.

Today you will place the windows and inside doorways. Remember, you are looking down on the rooms, but it will not be necessary to draw in the tables and chairs. You may add these elements to previous sketches or redraw your sketch below, fixing any mistakes before adding the new elements.

Using your sketch as a model, make a neat floor plan because you will be using it for the next two exercises. It would be good if you were to use a ruler to make straight lines. You will want to write the name of the room in the center of each one. You should write the word "North" at the top of the page. Be sure to save this page for the next two exercises.

Fill out the "Student Progress Report" on the next page.

Remember to fill out the writing skills mastery check-off form and, if necessary, to record spelling words and other problems that you need to address in the future.

CONTINUED ON NEXT PAGE→

Student Progress Report

This is the best sentence I wrote this week:

_____

_____

_____

_____

I think it is the best because:

_____

_____

_____

_____

I made this mistake this week, and this is what I learned to help me
avoid making the mistake again:

_____

_____

_____

_____

This is the sentence showing how I fixed this mistake:

_____

_____

_____

_____

Comments:

_____

_____

_____

_____

Your teacher will assign a book for you to read this week. Be sure to finish it before the end of the week. Review the five steps of reading literature and prepare to describe each of the five elements from your book.

Name of the book: _____

Author of the book: _____

Read and discuss with your teacher

The resolution is when the plot finally ends. Everything that has been set up in the exposition, the complication, the rising action, the climax, and the falling action is finally resolved or taken care of in the resolution.

If the characters have been on a journey, the resolution is when they reach their destination. If the story has been about two characters not getting along, the resolution is when one of them wins a showdown or when the two of them work out their differences. There are as many different types of resolutions as there are stories, but resolutions are always about bringing the story to an end.

One thing to remember about resolutions is that they are not always happy and they are not always clear. Sometimes, the action will continue after the story has ended. Other times, it is not exactly clear what happens — the writer leaves it up to the reader to figure out what has happened. Nonetheless, even if the ending is not what you expect it to be, it still has brought that particular story to a concluding point.

Endings are an important part of the story. You should take time to think about why an author has chosen to end a story a particular way. Is there a reason why one character won and the other did not? Is there a reason why it is not clear what has happened? Is there a reason that events still seem to be happening in the story? These are all good things to think about once you finish reading a story.

Discussion Questions

Think about one of your favorite stories. What is the resolution? How do you know that is the resolution? Is the resolution final or does it seem like the story is still continuing? Is the resolution clear or is it left up to the reader to decide what happened? Do you like the resolution — why or why not?

Objectives:

❶ Learn about resolution in plots.

❷ Read the assigned Bible passage.

❸ Answer questions about the assigned Bible passage.

❹ Write a paragraph.

❺ Read and discuss an assigned book (teacher's choice).

Note: The resolution is when the plot finally ends.

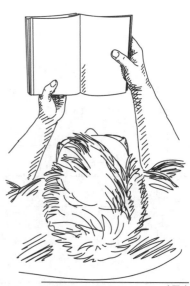

Read and discuss assigned passage

Read the following Bible passage: Jonah 3:1–4:11

Step One: Who is this passage about, and what is the cultural and historical setting?

_____

_____

_____

Step Two: What is the genre of this passage (history, poetry, prophecy, proverbs, letters, parables, etc.)?

_____

_____

_____

Step Three: What is the intended meaning of this passage? Some questions you can ask to help with this question are "What fallen or sinful condition is being highlighted in this passage?" or "What prompted the author to write this passage?" (Is this message about sin, salvation, faith, hope, etc.?)

_____

_____

_____

Step Four: Can you list other Bible passages that help define the intended meaning? (A concordance would be helpful here.)

_____

_____

_____

Step Five: Once the original meaning is understood, seek to find a simple life application.

_____

_____

_____

Read and discuss with your teacher

Answer the following questions about the passage:

1. What is the plot of this story (what are the events that happen)?

    _____

    _____

    _____

2. Does the story have a recognizable beginning, middle, and end? How do you know?

    _____

    _____

    _____

3. How does the plot connect with the story's theme? If you are not sure of what the story's theme is, think about the story's message. Does the plot connect to the message in some way?

    _____

    _____

    _____

4. What is the exposition? What is the complication? What is the rising action? What is the climax? What is the falling action?

    _____

    _____

    _____

Complete the following activity

Write a paragraph about the resolution of this week's passage. What is the resolution? Why do you think the story ends at that moment and not earlier? Why do you think it ends at that moment and not later?

_____

_____

_____

_____

_____

_____

_____

_____

_____

_____

_____

_____

_____

_____

Read and discuss assigned book

Remember to keep in mind these five principles when reading the book of your choice this week:

Step One: Determine the genre of the literature (historical fiction, fantasy, drama, Western, mystery, science fiction, poetry, biography, etc.).

_____

_____

_____

Step Two: Read the book, keeping in mind the main setting of the text and the primary roles of each character.

_____

_____

_____

Step Three: Look for the flow of the story. Describe the flow of the story from your book.

_____

_____

_____

Step Four: What is the book's message or what do you think it is trying to teach you?

_____

_____

_____

CONTINUED ON NEXT PAGE➜

Step Five: Does this message agree with what the Bible teaches? Why or why not?

_____

_____

_____

Prewriting

In the last exercise you drew a floor plan of your home. This is one way of describing something. Now you will describe your home using words. This time you will not have to walk through the house. You will be able to work from your floor plan.

Just as you started your floor plan with a general outline of the outside walls of the building, you will start your description with general statements about the building.

Introduction

Your teacher or parent may need to tell you a little of the information you will need for the introduction of your paper. Your introduction should include at least one sentence for each of the following:

1. The name of your house or apartment (The Smith House or The Smith Apartment)

_____

_____

2. Where it is located (The town it is in and the street it is on)

_____

_____

3. When it was built

_____

_____

4. How many rooms it has

_____

_____

Objectives:

❶ Understand the structure of description.

❷ Describe a building starting with general statements.

❸ Support general statements with detail.

❹ Turn graphic representations into verbal descriptions (drawings into words) so that someone else can make a floor plan from it.

❺ Study your own work and decide if it needs to be changed or made better.

❻ Add to or change your writing to make it better.

CONTINUED ON NEXT PAGE→

5. How many floors it has

_____

_____

6. How many people live in it

_____

_____

Writing: Body

The **first paragraph** of the **body** of your paper should contain the following:

1. A statement about the **shape and size** of your building or unit. When talking about shape, it might help your reader if you could describe the shape using shapes familiar to your reader: *My house is square or U-shaped*, or *My house is L-shaped.*

2. Your reader should be told about the **number of halls** there are and in which **direction they run**.

3. There should be a sentence that lists the **general areas** of the building and a statement about the **number of rooms** there are. This could sound like this:

   > In my home there are a number of areas: a large living room area, a kitchen and eating area, a formal dining room, a study and school room for homeschooling, a den for my parents, and a small garage.

4. Your reader should be told **where the major areas** in your home are. It might sound like this:

   > On the north side of the house, the front door opens into a short entryway that is next to the living room. The kitchen and breakfast room are in the back of the house on the south side. The bedrooms are on the east end of the building. That is where the sun can wake us up all summer.

DO NOT WRITE: "When you walk in the front door . . ." or "As you enter the den, on the right wall. . . ." You are not taking your reader on a tour of the house, you are just describing it.

Write your first paragraph:

_____

_____

_____

_____

_____

_____

_____

CONTINUED ON NEXT PAGE→

The **second paragraph** should describe the function of the rooms:
(Who spends time in them and what is done in them)

1. **How the rooms are used**. It might read like this:

   The big living room is mostly reserved for company. It has light-colored carpet in it and what we call "good furniture." When company comes or when we have a party at our house, we all use the living room.

2. The **bedrooms** part of your paper might read like this:

   The master bedroom is where my parents sleep. Dad has an exercise bike in there but the kids aren't allowed to use it. My brother has the small bedroom on the northeast corner of the house and I have the one next to it on the east side of the house.

3. When you write about the total number of rooms there are in the building, be sure you count the bathrooms and closets.

Write your second paragraph:

_____

_____

_____

_____

_____

_____

_____

_____

_____

_____

The **third paragraph of the body** should contain the following information:

1. **Where the closets are** in each of the rooms.

2. **Where the pantry or storage room is.**

3. **Where any special rooms are.** These could be rooms like the den, the laundry room, or the play room in the basement.

Write your third paragraph:

_____

_____

_____

_____

_____

_____

_____

_____

_____

_____

Conclusion

This paper needs a **conclusion**. A conclusion should do a number of things:

1. Tie all the ideas in the body together. In this paper the ideas in the body are:

   a. There are a lot of rooms in your home.

   b. It was designed so that the owners would find it easy to use. This part of the conclusion could sound like this:

   This house was very well designed. It is an easy building for my family to use because the places where we spend most of our time are near the outside doors.

CONTINUED ON NEXT PAGE➔

2. Make some **statement about what you think of your house**. It is not enough to say that you like it. What you say about your home must have something to do with the way it was designed and how it is used. This part could read this way:

> My home is like a fort to me. When I am home I feel really secure and safe. When I am with my family and we watch television or listen to the radio, I am always glad that I live in this house with these people. I often wish all kids could live in such a nice home.

Be creative and have fun with this exercise. Use your own ideas rather than my sentence structuring and my wording.

Write your concluding paragraph:

_____

_____

_____

_____

_____

_____

_____

_____

_____

_____

Now you will write your paper on the My Home Worksheet according to this setup.

HINT! Try to draw a floor plan of your house from your description of it.

Your Name

The Date

SPACE

SPACE

Your Title

SPACE

Introduction

Body   Do not label the parts of your paper nor skip lines between them

Conclusion

CONTINUED ON NEXT PAGE➜

CONTINUED ON NEXT PAGE →

_____

_____

_____

_____

_____

_____

_____

_____

_____

_____

_____

_____

_____

_____

_____

_____

_____

_____

_____

You have studied your home. You have made a floor plan of it. You have described your home with words. Now is the time for you to find out how well you have done.

Ask your teacher to give your "My Home, Part 2" paper to a neighbor or friend of the family. If this is not possible, your teacher might ask a family member to help. This person will use your word description of your house to try to draw a floor plan from it. **The teacher should tell the helper not to draw a floor plan from what that person remembers about your house. Only your descriptions may be used.**

If your description does not tell where something goes, it can be put anywhere. If you were not very careful with your description, you might get a floor plan back that has the kitchen in the middle of the living room.

When you get your description back, it will have a floor plan with it, and if it does not look like the floor plan you drew for the "My Home" exercise, that might mean that you made a mistake in the writing. Of course, the neighbor who made a floor plan from your description might not have known how to draw a floor plan from a description.

Writing

When you get your paper back, you will have to do one of the following two things:

1. You will have to give an explanation to your teacher of why there is a difference between the floor plan the neighbor drew from your description and the way your home really is; or,

2. You will have to explain to your teacher how you did everything just right so that the neighbor could draw a floor plan that looks just the way your house really is.

Write out either explanation below:

HINT! ⸙ This kind of exercise is hard. Even some high school kids have trouble with it. For some of us, it is not how we naturally think but we can get better at descriptions with practice.

_____

_____

_____

_____

_____

_____

_____

_____

_____

_____

Fill out the "Student Progress Report" on the next page.

Remember to fill out the writing skills mastery check-off form and, if necessary, to record spelling words and other problems that you need to address in the future.

Student Progress Report

This is the best sentence I wrote this week:

_____

_____

_____

_____

I think it is the best because:

_____

_____

_____

_____

I made this mistake this week and this is what I learned to help me avoid making the mistake again:

_____

_____

_____

_____

This is the sentence showing how I fixed the mistake:

_____

_____

_____

_____

Comments:

_____

_____

_____

_____

Your teacher will assign a book for you to read this week. Be sure to finish it before the end of the week. Review the five steps of reading literature and prepare to describe each of the five elements from your book.

Name of the book: _____

Author of the book: _____

Read and discuss with your teacher

We have covered all the most common elements of plot in Freytag's Pyramid: exposition, complication, rising action, climax, falling action, and resolution. These plot elements are all necessary for telling a good story.

1) The exposition gives us background to understand what will happen. 2) The complication gets the story started. 3) The rising action draws the reader in as more and more things happen with the characters. 4) The climax provides the most exciting part of the plot and decides how the story will end, though the readers probably still don't know what the ending will be. 5) The falling action ties everything together as the plot winds down. 6) The resolution ends the story.

Now that you have all the elements, you can see why the plot structure is called Freytag's Pyramid:

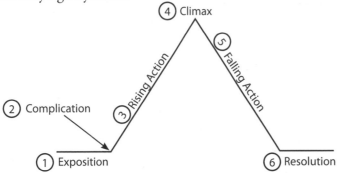

The tension in a story is what makes it fun to read. The amount of tension is determined by the plot elements. Most often, tension begins to build in the complication and increases with the rising action. The tension reaches its highest point in the climax and from there it starts to fall with the falling action. By the resolution, the tension is gone because the story has ended.

Discussion Questions

Think about one of the Bible passages we read earlier this year before we started looking at elements of plot. Who would you pick, Adam and Eve, Abraham and Isaac, Jacob and Esau, Joseph and his brothers, or Gideon? How would you divide the story into the different elements of plot and identify exposition, complication, rising action, climax, falling action, and resolution?

Objectives:

❶ Practice identifying the different elements of plot.

❷ Read the assigned Bible passage.

❸ Answer questions about the assigned Bible passage.

❹ Write a paragraph.

❺ Read and discuss the assigned book (teacher's choice).

Read and discuss assigned passage

Read the following Bible passage: John 11:1–44

Step One: Who is this passage about, and what is the cultural and historical setting?

_____

_____

_____

Step Two: What is the genre of this passage (history, poetry, prophecy, proverbs, letters, parables, etc.)?

_____

_____

_____

Step Three: What is the intended meaning of this passage? Some questions you can ask to help with this question are "What fallen or sinful condition is being highlighted in this passage?" or "What prompted the author to write this passage?" (Is this message about sin, salvation, faith, hope, etc.?)

_____

_____

_____

Step Four: Can you list other Bible passages that help define the intended meaning? (A concordance would be helpful here.)

_____

_____

_____

Step Five: Once the original meaning is understood, seek to find a simple life application.

_____

_____

_____

Read and discuss with your teacher

Answer the following questions about the passage:

1. What is the plot of this story (what are the events that happen)?

_____

_____

_____

2. Does the story have a recognizable beginning, middle, and end? How do you know?

_____

_____

_____

3. How does the plot connect with the story's theme? If you are not sure of what the story's theme is, think about the story's message. Does the plot connect to the message in some way?

_____

_____

_____

4. What is the exposition? What is the complication? What is the rising action? What is the climax? What is the falling action? What is the resolution?

_____

_____

_____

Complete the following activity

Pick one of the plot elements (exposition, complication, rising action, climax, falling action, resolution) and identify the part of the story from this week's Bible passage that is that plot element. Write a paragraph explaining how you know that part of the story is that plot element. Be sure to use specific examples and a topic sentence.

_____

_____

_____

_____

_____

_____

_____

_____

_____

_____

_____

_____

_____

_____

Read and discuss assigned book

Remember to keep in mind these five principles when reading the book of your choice this week:

Step One: Determine the genre of the literature (historical fiction, fantasy, drama, Western, mystery, science fiction, poetry, biography, etc.).

_____

_____

_____

Step Two: Read the book, keeping in mind the main setting of the text and the primary roles of each character.

_____

_____

_____

Step Three: Look for the flow of the story. Describe the flow of the story from your book.

_____

_____

_____

Step Four: What is the book's message or what do you think it is trying to teach you?

_____

_____

_____

Step Five: Does this message agree with what the Bible teaches? Why or why not?

_____

_____

_____

Prewriting

Describing a thing is not too hard because you can look at it and say what it looks like. If it is small enough, you can even pick it up and describe what it feels like and tell how heavy it is. Think of model cars and oranges.

What is hard to do is to describe a problem. That is why it is so much fun. We will work together on a thought problem.

Let's start our problem with the words *what if*. Now all we have to do is think of a problem and introduce it with those words. Here are some possibilities.

Objectives:

❶ Picture a situation in your mind which would be a problem.

❷ Describe what such an imaginary situation would be like.

❸ Solve a thought problem.

1. **What if** there were no more books?

_____

_____

_____

2. **What if** one morning none of the engines in any of the cars, trucks, or buses would run?

_____

_____

_____

3. **What if** one day people had no thumbs?

_____

_____

_____

4. **What if** all the people in the world woke up one morning and they were all the same color?

_____

_____

_____

CONTINUED ON NEXT PAGE➔

5. **What if** people or cats or dogs could fly?

_____

_____

_____

Spend time writing some of your own "what if" questions.

_____

_____

_____

_____

_____

_____

_____

_____

_____

_____

_____

There is no end to the possibilities for thought problems. It gets fun to think of all the things that would have to change or be done with some of the "what if" problems. I will choose a problem and we will work through it together.

> What if, one morning, the public library were floating two feet off the ground?

That is crazy, is it not? But, that is why it is fun. The first thing we will have to do is describe what the building would look like floating in the air, and then we will have to solve the problems this would cause. So, this exercise will have two parts:

Part 1. Describe a thought problem as if it were real

Part 2. Solve the thought problem

To do this we will have to:

1. **See the floating library** in our minds

2. **Describe** in detail what we see

3. Tell what the **people would do** in this situation

4. Decide how the **people could solve** the problem

5. **Describe the solving** of the problem

Very few buildings float, so we will have to be creative and use our imaginations.

We will write this in **past tense**, except for the **last sentence** which will be in the present tense. I am going to write the whole exercise as an example just as if I were doing it.

The Floating Library

When we went to the library on Monday morning to get more books for reading, the building was floating two feet off the ground. Even the front lawn, the sidewalks and the night depository stand were floating. Kids were jumping off the lawn onto the street and then climbing back up onto the library property. Some of the librarians were having trouble clambering up onto the high sidewalks.

CONTINUED ON NEXT PAGE➜

When the head librarian came to work, he put a box on the edge of the walk so others could get into the building. The mayor came in a police car to find out what all the excitement was about. That afternoon she called a meeting of the city council to see what could be done about the floating library.

The mayor and the council invited anyone who wanted to come to the meeting to do so and tell what they thought could be done to get the building back down. The mayor and all the important people in town decided that the library was too light and that was why it was floating. They thought that if they made the building darker it might settle back down.

They painted all the windows with black paint. As soon as this was done the library started to lower. When the mayor told the head librarian to turn off all the lights in the building, the library dropped down with a plop.

The mayor explained the problem in the paper the next day. She said that the library had too much light reading in it. She told the head librarian to order some heavy reading. She said that when this was done it would anchor the building and give it a good foundation.

Once the problem was solved, we could go back to the library to read and get books. Only now the books are so heavy, we have to take a wheelbarrow to bring any home, and, if we want to read the books there, we have to take a flashlight.

HINT! Examples of puns:

What do you call a sleeping bull? A bulldozer.

My fear of moving stairs is escalating.

You should recognize that some of the words I chose were used in a punning way. Puns use words that have two meanings. See if you can spot them. Circle them and then tell your teacher how I distorted the ideas in the writing by using puns.

Writing

Start your mind working on the *What if* sentence. If you cannot think of one, use one of my suggestions listed on the first page of this exercise. As soon as you have selected a problem, picture it in your mind; then you will be ready to write.

Use this outline to help you organize your thinking:

1. **Describe the problem** in **past tense.**

_____

_____

_____

_____

_____

2. Tell how the **people acted.**

_____

_____

_____

_____

_____

3. Tell how **they tried to solve** the problem.

_____

_____

_____

_____

_____

CONTINUED ON NEXT PAGE➔

4. Explain how the **problem was solved.**

_____

_____

_____

_____

_____

5. Tell **what it is like <u>now</u>** after the problem **has been** solved. (Use **present tense** for this last step.)

_____

_____

_____

_____

_____

Writing
Lesson 13

Day 124

Describing a Thought Problem
Organization

Name

Write your paper below, following the example.

Your Name

The Date

SPACE

SPACE

Your Title

SPACE

Start your paper here with the problem described in past tense

What the situation was like because of the thought problem

What the people or person did to solve the thought problem

What it is like now that the problem has been solved - Do this in present tense

_____

_____

_____

_____

_____

_____

_____

_____

_____

_____

_____

_____

_____

Read your paper that you wrote yesterday to your class or to a family member. Ask them if they have ever thought of a fun "what if" question and if so, to share it with you.

Fill out the "Student Progress Report" on the next page.

Remember to fill out the writing skills mastery check-off form and, if necessary, to record spelling words and other problems that you need to address in the future.

CONTINUED ON NEXT PAGE →

Student Progress Report

This is the best sentence I wrote this week:

_____

_____

_____

_____

I think it is the best because:

_____

_____

_____

_____

I made this mistake this week and this is what I learned to help me
avoid making the mistake again:

_____

_____

_____

_____

This is the sentence showing how I fixed the mistake:

_____

_____

_____

_____

Comments:

_____

_____

_____

_____

Your teacher will assign a book for you to read this week. Be sure to finish it before the end of the week. Review the five steps of reading literature and prepare to describe each of the five elements from your book.

Name of the book: _____

Author of the book: _____

Read and discuss with your teacher

We've spent a long time studying the elements of plot and how to break a story down into several different parts. Understanding how stories work help us better appreciate them.

Another important aspect of plot is conflict. You might have realized this while we studied plot elements. Plots do not work without tension, and there is no tension in a story if there is no conflict.

There are several different types of conflict in literature. We are going to be studying them for the next few Reading Lessons. Conflict can be divided into two general types: external and internal. We'll cover internal more later, but conflict can come from the main character being in conflict with something or someone else (external) or from being in conflict with one's self (internal).

There are several basic types of external conflict in stories, but one of the most common is conflict between characters. The main character may have a main opponent, the antagonist of the story. The main character may be in conflict with several people. But the driving force of the plot of such a story will revolve around this conflict, the tension that results from it, and how the conflict is resolved. Maybe the characters become friends or have a fight and one wins.

Discussion Questions

Think about one of your favorite stories. Who is the main character? What other character is this main character in conflict with? How important is this conflict to the plot? How is this conflict resolved?

Objectives:

❶ Learn about the importance of conflict in plots.

❷ Read the assigned Bible passage.

❸ Answer questions about the assigned Bible passage.

❹ Write a paragraph.

❺ Read and discuss an assigned book (teacher's choice).

HINT! Plots do not work without tension, and there is no tension in a story if there is no conflict.

Read and discuss assigned passage

Read the following Bible passage: Luke 4:14–30

Step One: Who is this passage about, and what is the cultural and historical setting?

_____

_____

_____

Step Two: What is the genre of this passage (history, poetry, prophecy, proverbs, letters, parables, etc.)?

_____

_____

_____

Step Three: What is the intended meaning of this passage? Some questions you can ask to help with this question are "What fallen or sinful condition is being highlighted in this passage?" or "What prompted the author to write this passage?" (Is this message about sin, salvation, faith, hope, etc.?)

_____

_____

_____

Step Four: Can you list other Bible passages that help define the intended meaning? (A concordance would be helpful here.)

_____

_____

_____

Step Five: Once the original meaning is understood, seek to find a simple life application.

_____

_____

_____

Read and discuss with your teacher

Answer the following questions about the passage:

1. What is the plot of this story (what are the events that happen)?

_____

_____

_____

2. Does the story have a recognizable beginning, middle, and end? How do you know?

_____

_____

_____

3. How does the plot connect with the story's theme? If you are not sure of what the story's theme is, think about the story's message. Does the plot connect to the message in some way?

_____

_____

_____

4. What is the exposition? What is the complication? What is the rising action? What is the climax? What is the falling action? What is the resolution?

_____

_____

_____

Complete the following activity

What conflict with other people does Jesus encounter in this passage? Why do you think He says that prophets are always rejected in their hometowns? What effect does this conflict have on the story? Would there be a story without this conflict? Write a paragraph that explains your answers. Be sure that your paragraph is well organized and includes a topic sentence and specific examples.

_____

_____

_____

_____

_____

_____

_____

_____

_____

_____

_____

_____

_____

_____

_____

Read and discuss assigned book

Remember to keep in mind these five principles when reading the book of your choice this week:

Step One: Determine the genre of the literature (historical fiction, fantasy, drama, Western, mystery, science fiction, poetry, biography, etc.).

_____

_____

_____

Step Two: Read the book, keeping in mind the main setting of the text and the primary roles of each character.

_____

_____

_____

Step Three: Look for the flow of the story. Describe the flow of the story from your book.

_____

_____

_____

Step Four: What is the book's message or what do you think it is trying to teach you?

_____

_____

_____

Step Five: Does this message agree with what the Bible teaches? Why or why not?

_____

_____

_____

Prewriting

As an example of how objects change, think of a peach. Before it is picked, it is small, hard and light green in color. When it is ripe enough to be picked, it is full of juice, bright yellow and peach-colored, and soft. When it has been sitting on a shelf for two weeks, it has large, brown rotten spots on it. Its skin has begun to dry and wrinkle.

For this exercise, ask your teacher for two pieces of fruit, one fresh and one that is starting to rot. You will describe these two pieces of fruit as if they were the same piece but examined at different times:

First description: When it is ready to eat

Second description: After it has been sitting on a shelf too long

You will need an introduction for this paper. An introduction gives background information to the reader and identifies the main idea of your paper. It should be interesting enough that people want to continue reading your paper.

Your **introduction for this paper will have three points:**

1. **An experience** that started you thinking about how some things change

2. **A decision** to examine change in an organized way

3. **A mention of the object** you used to examine the ways things change

In this introduction, you will write about the above three points. Below is a short list of possibilities for the introduction. You cannot use my wording or situation in your paper.

First point for the introduction:

> My father and I stopped at our minister's house to wish him a happy birthday. He was in the garden pulling weeds. We stood at one end of a row of sweet corn and talked to him for a few minutes. I was impressed with how dirty his clothes were. His knees had dark patches of dirt on them and his shirt was dirty where he had wiped his face against it, clearing the sweat out of his eyes. This was the first time I had ever seen him when he wasn't neat and clean.

Second point for the introduction:

> I was so impressed by this change in his appearance that I thought about how all things must change, and I decided to look

Objectives:

❶ Learn that things do change.

❷ Understand that descriptions of changes can be organized.

❸ Describe changes so they are easy to understand.

❹ Write a paper that has an introduction and a conclusion.

HINT! In some introductions you can use an experience you have had that caused you to think about the subject.

CONTINUED ON NEXT PAGE→

at the process of change. But, I knew I would not understand much about change unless I made an organized examination.

Third point for the introduction:

I chose to examine a peach and watch it as it rotted. I set one on the windowsill in the kitchen and took notes as it rotted.

The three parts of the introduction should be combined into one paragraph.

Writing

Begin your introduction by telling your reader that you had an experience where something had changed. This made you realize that many things can change in appearance. To study this idea, you took a piece of fruit and examined it at different times to see the progression of changes in physical characteristics.

Make sure your teacher has a chance to read your introduction before you are done studying writing for today.

_____

_____

_____

_____

_____

_____

_____

Rewrite your introduction using the suggestions your teacher has given you.

_____

_____

_____

_____

_____

_____

_____

When you describe how something has changed, you can write about how it looks and how it feels. In this case, you will not want to describe how the rotten fruit tastes.

When you write about how the fruit **looks**, you can write about:

1. Color

2. Size

3. Shape

4. Texture

When you write about how the fruit **feels**, you can write about:

1. Smoothness

2. Wetness or dryness

3. Softness or firmness

4. Weight

Today you will write about how the fresh fruit **looks**. There should be at least two or three sentences about each of the conditions in the above list on appearance. When you are finished, show it to your teacher for suggestions.

_____

_____

_____

_____

_____

_____

_____

_____

_____

_____

_____

_____

CONTINUED ON NEXT PAGE➔

Using your teacher's suggestions, rewrite your paragraph about how the fresh fruit looks and show it to your teacher.

_____

_____

_____

_____

_____

_____

Write about how the fresh fruit feels. Again, there should be at least two or three sentences about each of the conditions in the list of how things feel. Show your paragraph to your teacher.

_____

_____

_____

_____

_____

_____

You should use your teacher's suggestions and rewrite your paragraph about how the fresh fruit feels and show it to your teacher.

_____

_____

_____

_____

_____

_____

You will write about how the rotten fruit looks. Ask your teacher to give you suggestions about how to improve your work.

_____

_____

_____

_____

_____

_____

_____

Rewrite your paragraph about how the rotten fruit looks and show it to your teacher.

_____

_____

_____

_____

_____

_____

_____

Write your paragraph about how the rotten fruit feels. Show your paragraph to your teacher and ask for suggestions.

_____

_____

_____

_____

_____

_____

CONTINUED ON NEXT PAGE➔

Rewrite your paragraph about how the rotten fruit **feels**.

_____

_____

_____

_____

_____

_____

_____

Your **conclusion** should have three points as listed below:

Point 1. Mention the observation which caused you to think about how things change. (But don't write the whole thing over again.)

Point 2. Tell your reader what you have learned from observing how things change.

Point 3. Mention that now you will be looking for signs of change.

Conclusions are harder to write than introductions. I will demonstrate how to write one using the above three points.

Example Conclusion:

> **Point 1.** I am surprised when I think that this whole examination started with my minister weeding his corn. **Point 2.** But, I am glad we stopped by on his birthday because I ended up learning a lot about the need to organize my thinking when I want to find out about things. **Point 3.** I realize from this that almost everything changes, and I will watch for signs of this everywhere now.

(You cannot use my wording in your papers. You can use the structure of the paragraphs, though.)

_____

_____

_____

_____

_____

_____

_____

_____

_____

Prepare your whole paper on the Worksheet to present to your teacher.
Use this chart.

> Your Name
>
> The Date
>
> SPACE
>
> SPACE
>
> Your Title
>
> SPACE

INTRODUCTION

Point 1

Point 2

Point 3

BODY

Fresh Fruit

      Looks

      Feels

Rotten Fruit

      Looks

      Feels

CONCLUSION

Point 1

Point 2

Point 3

CONTINUED ON NEXT PAGE →

_____

_____

_____

_____

_____

_____

_____

_____

_____

_____

_____

_____

_____

_____

_____

_____

_____

_____

_____

_____

_____

_____

_____

_____

_____

_____

_____

Fill out the "Student Progress Report" on the next page.

Remember to fill out the writing skills mastery check-off form and, if necessary, to record spelling words and other problems that you need to address in the future.

Student Progress Report

This is the best sentence I wrote this week:

_____

_____

_____

_____

I think it is the best because:

_____

_____

_____

_____

I made this mistake this week and this is what I learned to help me
avoid making the mistake again:

_____

_____

_____

_____

This is the sentence showing how I fixed the mistake:

_____

_____

_____

_____

Comments:

_____

_____

_____

_____

Your teacher will assign a book for you to read this week. Be sure to finish it before the end of the week. Review the five steps of reading literature and prepare to describe each of the five elements from your book.

Name of the book: _____

Author of the book: _____

Read and discuss with your teacher

Though conflict between individuals is one of the most common forms of conflict in stories, a lot of plots also derive their tension from conflict between a main character and society. In these plots, the main character may be at odds with the government or the culture of the setting.

The basic principles are the same as conflict between individuals, though. In stories that focus on conflict between societies and individuals, the tension that sparks the complication and fuels the rising action, climax, and falling action and is solved in the resolution derives from this struggle.

Discussion Questions

Think about a story you have read that involved a character in conflict with society. Who was the character? What society was he or she in conflict with? How important is this conflict to the plot? How is this conflict resolved?

Objectives:

❶ Learn about conflict in plots.

❷ Read the assigned Bible passage.

❸ Answer questions about the assigned Bible passage.

❹ Write a letter.

❺ Read and discuss an assigned book (teacher's choice).

Read and discuss assigned passage

Read the following Bible passage: John 9:1–41

Step One: Who is this passage about, and what is the cultural and historical setting?

_____

_____

_____

Step Two: What is the genre of this passage (history, poetry, prophecy, proverbs, letters, parables, etc.)?

_____

_____

_____

Step Three: What is the intended meaning of this passage? Some questions you can ask to help with this question are "What fallen or sinful condition is being highlighted in this passage?" or "What prompted the author to write this passage?" (Is this message about sin, salvation, faith, hope, etc.?)

_____

_____

_____

Step Four: Can you list other Bible passages that help define the intended meaning? (A concordance would be helpful here.)

_____

_____

_____

Step Five: Once the original meaning is understood, seek to find a simple life application.

_____

_____

_____

Read and discuss with your teacher

Answer the following questions about the passage:

1. What is the plot of this story (what are the events that happen)?

_____

_____

_____

2. Does the story have a recognizable beginning, middle, and end?
   How do you know?

_____

_____

_____

3. How does the plot connect with the story's theme? If you are not
   sure of what the story's theme is, think about the story's message.
   Does the plot connect to the message in some way?

_____

_____

_____

4. What is the exposition? What is the complication? What is the rising
   action? What is the climax? What is the falling action? What is the
   resolution?

_____

_____

_____

Complete the following activity

What conflict does the blind man have with society? Think about how other characters, including both the Pharisees and the disciples, think about blindness. What effect does this conflict have on the story? Would there be a story without this conflict? Write a paragraph that explains your answers. Be sure that your paragraph is well organized and includes a topic sentence and specific examples.

_____

_____

_____

_____

_____

_____

_____

_____

_____

_____

_____

_____

_____

_____

_____

_____

Read and discuss assigned book

Remember to keep in mind these five principles when reading the book of your choice this week:

Step One: Determine the genre of the literature (historical fiction, fantasy, drama, Western, mystery, science fiction, poetry, biography, etc.).

_____

_____

_____

Step Two: Read the book, keeping in mind the main setting of the text and the primary roles of each character.

_____

_____

_____

Step Three: Look for the flow of the story. Describe the flow of the story from your book.

_____

_____

_____

Step Four: What is the book's message or what do you think it is trying to teach you?

_____

_____

_____

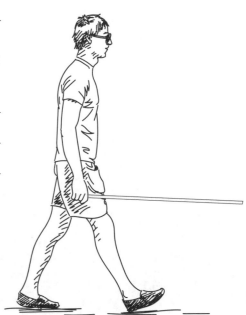

CONTINUED ON NEXT PAGE➔

Step Five: Does this message agree with what the Bible teaches? Why or why not?

_____

_____

_____

Writing
Lesson 15

Day 141

From Where I Was
Creative

Name

Prewriting

When the narrative voice is a character speaking in first person, that character has to be in some real place in the story — in the backyard, sitting at a table, riding a bus, etc.

Where the character is (their position) determines what that character can see and understand about the action that is taking place in the story.

You are to write two accounts of the same event, where two different characters in your story view the same action from a different position. (An account is simply a description of a past event.) You should write both accounts in first person.

It will help you to write these two accounts if you read through my example before you begin. Your paper should contain:

1. **The positions of the characters** in your action

2. **A scenario.** (A scenario is just a summary or synopsis of the scene. It should be written in third person and present tense.)

3. **The first account** of the event as told by one of the characters in past tense

4. **The second account** of the same event as told by another character in present tense.

Example

#1. Character Positions

Character A. Bill is in the back of the garage behind a large workbench. He is looking under the bench for a wrench he dropped.

Character B. Janet is inside a large playhouse inside the garage. She made the playhouse from an old refrigerator box and can see out of a small window cut in the side of the box.

Character C. Mr. Roberts has backed the family station wagon up to the garage and is unloading it.

Objectives:

❶ Understand that characters in fiction must be in specific places.

❷ Understand that position (place) determines what characters can experience.

❸ Understand that you can control the position of your first person narrative voice characters.

HINT! Think of yourself as a character in a piece of fiction. What can you know from where you are?

CONTINUED ON NEXT PAGE➔

#2. Scenario (third person, present tense)

It is Bill's birthday and Mr. Roberts has bought him a new ten-speed mountain bike. He backs the family station wagon up to the garage and looks around to be sure that Bill will not see him unload the bike.

Janet is in her refrigerator-box playhouse and watches her father unload a new blue bike from the car. She has seen Bill come into the garage but does not know if he has seen their father with the bike and says nothing.

Bill has heard the car drive up, but he is looking for a wrench he has dropped under the work bench at the back of the garage, and, looking upside-down at the world, sees a bike being unloaded.

#3. First Account — Janet (past tense):

I was inside my playhouse when I heard Bill come into the garage. I knew it was him `cause I could hear his whistling. Nobody whistles the way Bill does; there is no tune at all. He just makes this whistling sound between his teeth, both in and out. It really gets on my nerves sometimes.

He was in the back of the garage and Dad backed up to the door with the car and unloaded a new bike. It was just what Bill's been asking for. I watched out the window I cut in the box. I do not think anybody knew I was there at all.

#4. Second Account — Bill (present tense):

I have to find a wrench to tighten the hose on the faucet. Dad does not like it to drip and run down the driveway. I know Janet is in the box in the garage as soon as I walk in. I can hear her talking to her dolls. I start that whistling I know bugs her just to let her know I know she is there. Just as I find the wrench, I drop it under the bench, and, at the same time, Dad backs the car up to the garage. He gets out and looks around like he is afraid of being seen. I have to look at all this between the shelves and hanging upside-down because I am leaning over the back of the bench reaching down trying to get my fingers on the wrench. I do not think he even sees me. Then he unloads the neatest bike! It is all I can do not to yell out.

Writing

Step #1. Review how to create the **position** of your characters. You will have to plan what you are going to write about before you begin to write. It may help you to make notes on other paper. You can write about an incident that has happened to you, or just make one up.

Write your **Character Positions**:

_____

_____

_____

_____

_____

_____

_____

_____

_____

_____

_____

_____

_____

_____

_____

_____

Ask your teacher to read what you have written.

Step #2. Review how to write your **scenario**.

Write your **Scenario**:

_____

_____

_____

_____

_____   ***HINT!*** Remember to
write your scenario in third
_____   person and present tense.

_____

_____

_____

_____

_____

_____

_____

_____

Rewrite your rough draft using your teacher's suggestions.

_____

_____

_____

_____

_____

_____

_____

_____

Step #3. Review Step #3 then write the **First Account** of the event as told in first person and past tense by one of the characters.

_____

_____

_____

_____

_____

_____

_____

_____

When you have the rough draft finished, ask your teacher to give you suggestions.

Rewrite your rough draft using your teacher's suggestions.

_____

_____

_____

_____

_____

_____

_____

_____

_____

Step #4. Review and write the **Second Account** as told by another character in first person and in present tense. When you are finished, ask your teacher for suggestions.

_____

_____

_____

_____

_____

_____

_____

_____

_____

Rewrite the second account and give it to your teacher.

_____

_____

_____

_____

_____

_____

_____

_____

_____

Fill out the "Student Progress Report" on the next page.

Remember to fill out the writing skills mastery check-off form and, if necessary, to record spelling words and other problems that you need to address in the future.

From Where I Was Creative	Name

Student Progress Report

This is the best sentence I wrote this week:

_____

_____

_____

_____

I think it is the best because:

_____

_____

_____

_____

I made this mistake this week and this is what I learned to help me avoid making the mistake again:

_____

_____

_____

_____

This is the sentence showing how I fixed the mistake:

_____

_____

_____

_____

Comments:

_____

_____

_____

_____

Your teacher will assign a book for you to read this week. Be sure to finish it before the end of the week. Review the five steps of reading literature and prepare to describe each of the five elements from your book.

Name of the book: _____

Author of the book: _____

Read and discuss with your teacher

Characters can be at conflict with others or with society, but they can also be in conflict with nature or their setting. If you did *Writing Strands Beginning 2*, you might remember that we did some lessons on conflict with setting. The difference between a conflict with society and a conflict with the setting is that the conflict with setting involves a conflict with the actual physical environment.

Maybe the character is battling a storm or is in a difficult environment, like a desert. This type of conflict usually involves a character being in conflict with the natural world, but perhaps the character is in conflict with something man-made, like a building or a boat.

Just like other forms of conflict, this one can provide the tension necessary for a plot to sustain reader interest and create a compelling plot.

Discussion Questions

Can you think of any stories you have read that involve a conflict between the character and the setting? Who is the character? What is the setting he or she is in conflict with? How important is this conflict to the plot? How is this conflict resolved?

Objectives:

❶ Learn about conflict in plots.

❷ Read the assigned Bible passage.

❸ Answer questions about the assigned Bible passage.

❹ Write a paragraph.

❺ Read and discuss an assigned book (teacher's choice).

Read and discuss assigned passage

Read the following Bible passage: Luke 5:17–26

Step One: Who is this passage about, and what is the cultural and historical setting?

_____

_____

_____

Step Two: What is the genre of this passage (history, poetry, prophecy, proverbs, letters, parables, etc.)?

_____

_____

_____

Step Three: What is the intended meaning of this passage? Some questions you can ask to help with this question are "What fallen or sinful condition is being highlighted in this passage?" or "What prompted the author to write this passage?" (Is this message about sin, salvation, faith, hope, etc.?)

_____

_____

_____

Step Four: Can you list other Bible passages that help define the intended meaning? (A concordance would be helpful here.)

_____

_____

_____

Step Five: Once the original meaning is understood, seek to find a simple life application.

_____

_____

_____

Read and discuss with your teacher

Answer the following questions about the passage:

1. What is the plot of this story (what are the events that happen)?

_____

_____

_____

2. Does the story have a recognizable beginning, middle, and end? How do you know?

_____

_____

_____

3. How does the plot connect with the story's theme? If you are not sure of what the story's theme is, think about the story's message. Does the plot connect to the message in some way?

_____

_____

_____

4. What is the exposition? What is the complication? What is the rising action? What is the climax? What is the falling action? What is the resolution?

_____

_____

_____

Complete the following activity

There are all sorts of conflict in this story. What is the conflict between the paralyzed man's friends and the setting? What is the conflict between Jesus and the Pharisees? How are these conflicts similar? How are they different? What is the effect of including both of these conflicts in the story?

Write a short, well-organized, 4-paragraph essay that answers these questions.

Identify the types of conflict you are going to talk about and your thoughts on the subject in the introduction. Write about the conflict between the paralyzed man's friends and the setting in the second paragraph. Write about the conflict between Jesus and the Pharisees in the third paragraph, and wrap up your essay with a concluding paragraph.

_____

_____

_____

_____

_____

_____

_____

_____

_____

_____

_____

_____

_____

_____

_____

_____

_____

_____

Read and discuss assigned book

Remember to keep in mind these five principles when reading the book of your choice this week:

Step One: Determine the genre of the literature (historical fiction, fantasy, drama, Western, mystery, science fiction, poetry, biography, etc.).

_____

_____

_____

Step Two: Read the book, keeping in mind the main setting of the text and the primary roles of each character.

_____

_____

_____

Step Three: Look for the flow of the story. Describe the flow of the story from your book.

_____

_____

_____

Step Four: What is the book's message or what do you think it is trying to teach you?

_____

_____

_____

Step Five: Does this message agree with what the Bible teaches? Why or why not?

_____

_____

_____

Prewriting

One of the major jobs authors have is controlling the feelings of their readers. There are many ways authors do this, and one of the easiest to understand is to examine the ways they describe objects and situations.

In this exercise, you will describe a situation **two times**.

The **first** time you will make your reader like it.

The **second** time you will make your reader dislike it.

First description: You will write about a picnic as if you are a mother who loves all kids. You must make your reader enjoy all of the things the mother sees, hears, and smells. If you use the following list it may help:

Objectives:

❶ Understand that authors give attitudes to their narrative voices.

❷ Understand that you can give your reader feelings by the attitudes you give your first-person characters.

She Sees:

1. The bright colors of the clothing

2. The fast movements of the excited kids

3. The fixing and eating of hot dogs and desserts

4. The laughing and smiling faces

5. The eagerness of the kids to be together

6. The fun the kids have running and playing

7. The other mothers laughing and talking with the kids

She Hears:

1. The loud laughter and talking

2. The rustle and pop of paper bags and soda cans

3. The bang and crash of silverware

4. The noise of speedboats on the lake

She Smells:

1. The pickles and mustard

2. The charcoal fire and the broiling hot dogs

3. The flowers growing nearby

CONTINUED ON NEXT PAGE→

Writing

The example below illustrates how it is possible to show how a character might be feeling about an event or a place:

It's a beautiful summer day, and I can smell the jasmine growing on the fence next to the slide. As I help some of the younger kids climb the slide's ladder, I realize I have lost track of my own son. I look up, and the picnic area is just a sea of color. There are children everywhere. Now, what color is Bill's shirt? I think it is blue. There must be dozens of boys with blue on.

I hear the humming of a boat motor and look toward the water, seeing the wake waves wash over some kids who are swimming. Has Bill gone swimming? Is he out too far? Worried, I start walking toward the water when I notice the scent of hot dogs grilling. Sure enough, I find Bill standing in line for a hot dog. I should have known where he would be.

Write a rough draft of what the mother sees using your own words. Remember, your reader should feel that the mother likes what she is seeing. This should be written in first person and present tense.

_____

_____

_____

_____

_____

_____

_____

_____

_____

Be sure your teacher reads what you have written.

Rewrite your rough draft of what the mother sees using your teacher's suggestions.

_____

_____

_____

_____

_____

_____

_____

_____

_____

Write a rough draft of what the mother hears. Keep in mind that the mother likes what she hears and so should the reader.

_____

_____

_____

_____

_____

_____

_____

_____

_____

Rewrite your rough draft using your teacher's suggestions.

_____

_____

_____

_____

_____

_____

_____

_____

_____

Write a rough draft of what the mother smells. Remember to use first person and present tense.

_____

_____

_____

_____

_____

_____

_____

_____

_____

Rewrite your rough draft using your teacher's suggestions.

_____

_____

_____

_____

_____

_____

_____

_____

_____

_____

Now put it all together. Write a finished copy of what the mother sees, hears, and smells.

_____

_____

_____

_____

_____

_____

_____

_____

_____

_____

_____

_____

_____

_____

_____

_____

_____

_____

_____

Fill out the "Student Progress Report" on the next page.

Remember to fill out the writing skills mastery check-off form and, if necessary, to record spelling words and other problems that you need to address in the future.

Student Progress Report

This is the best sentence I wrote this week

_____

_____

_____

_____

I think it is the best because:

_____

_____

_____

_____

I made this mistake this week and this is what I learned to help me
avoid making the mistake again:

_____

_____

_____

_____

This is the sentence showing how I fixed the mistake:

_____

_____

_____

_____

Comments:

_____

_____

_____

_____

Reading
Lesson 16

Day
156

Plot
Internal Conflict

Name

Your teacher will assign a book for you to read this week. Be sure to finish it before the end of the week. Review the five steps of reading literature and prepare to describe each of the five elements from your book.

Name of the book: _____

Author of the book: _____

Read and discuss with your teacher

We have studied how important conflict is to the plot in stories, but not all conflict takes place between a character and something or someone else. Sometimes, the primary conflict is internal for a character. In these stories, the tension that drives the conflict is because the character is torn between two decisions or is conflicted about something.

Do you remember learning about the driving forces of plots earlier this year? A plot-driven story is more likely to be about conflict between a character and another character or a character versus society or a character versus nature. But character-driven stories are more likely to be about a character's internal conflict.

Discussion Question

Can you think of a story you have read that is about a character's internal conflict? Who was the character? What was the conflict? How important was this conflict to the plot? How was the conflict resolved?

Objectives:

❶ Learn about conflict in plots.

❷ Read the assigned Bible passage.

❸ Answer questions about the assigned Bible passage.

❹ Write a paragraph.

❺ Read and discuss an assigned book (teacher's choice).

HINT! Sometimes, the primary conflict is internal for a character.

Read and discuss assigned passage

Read the following Bible passage: Luke 22:39–62

Step One: Who is this passage about, and what is the cultural and historical setting?

_____

_____

_____

Step Two: What is the genre of this passage (history, poetry, prophecy, proverbs, letters, parables, etc.)?

_____

_____

_____

Step Three: What is the intended meaning of this passage? Some questions you can ask to help with this question are "What fallen or sinful condition is being highlighted in this passage?" or "What prompted the author to write this passage?" (Is this message about sin, salvation, faith, hope, etc.?)

_____

_____

_____

Step Four: Can you list other Bible passages that help define the intended meaning? (A concordance would be helpful here.)

_____

_____

_____

Step Five: Once the original meaning is understood, seek to find a simple life application.

_____

_____

Read and discuss with your teacher

Answer the following questions about the passage:

1. What is the plot of this story (what are the events that happen)?

_____

_____

_____

2. Does the story have a recognizable beginning, middle, and end? How do you know?

_____

_____

_____

3. How does the plot connect with the story's theme? If you are not sure of what the story's theme is, think about the story's message. Does the plot connect to the message in some way?

_____

_____

_____

4. What is the exposition? What is the complication? What is the rising action? What is the climax? What is the falling action? What is the resolution?

_____

_____

_____

Complete the following activity

There are two different characters going through internal conflict in this passage. One is Jesus when He is praying in the garden and one is Peter as he is denying Jesus. Pick one of these moments and write a short, well-organized essay that answers the following questions: What is the internal conflict the character is experiencing? How does this internal conflict create tension in the plot? How is this different from a story about external conflict? How is the internal conflict resolved?

In your introduction, identify the character and the internal conflict you are going to talk about and your thoughts on the subject. Then, answer the above questions in the next two paragraphs and wrap it up with a concluding paragraph.

_____

_____

_____

_____

_____

_____

_____

_____

_____

_____

_____

_____

_____

_____

_____

_____

_____

Read and discuss assigned book

Remember to keep in mind these five principles when reading the book of your choice this week:

Step One: Determine the genre of the literature (historical fiction, fantasy, drama, Western, mystery, science fiction, poetry, biography, etc.).

_____

_____

_____

Step Two: Read the book, keeping in mind the main setting of the text and the primary roles of each character.

_____

_____

_____

Step Three: Look for the flow of the story. Describe the flow of the story from your book.

_____

_____

_____

Step Four: What is the book's message or what do you think it is trying to teach you?

_____

_____

_____

Step Five: Does this message agree with what the Bible teaches? Why or why not?

_____

_____

_____

Writing

Second description: Now you will write about the picnic as if it were being described by the groundskeeper who has to clean up after the picnic. You should use the same list, except the man will see and hear things differently from how the mother does. Your reader should understand that the man does not like what he sees and hears. Use first person and present tense.

Objectives:

❶ Understand that authors give attitudes to their narrative voices.

❷ Understand that you can give your reader feelings by the attitudes you give your first-person characters.

Example

What a mess. It looks like there is a war going on here. Every time I smell a barbecue grill, I know I will find paper napkins, pop cans, and all kinds of garbage lying around. I do not know why these parents cannot clean up after their own screaming kids. There is even ketchup on the swings! This is going to take a long time to clean up.

Using your own words, write a rough draft of what the man sees.

_____

_____

_____

_____

_____

_____

_____

_____

Rewrite your rough draft using your teacher's suggestions.

_____

_____

_____

_____

_____

_____

_____

Write a rough draft of what the man hears.

_____

_____

_____

_____

_____

_____

_____

_____

Rewrite your rough draft using your teacher's suggestions.

_____

_____

_____

_____

_____

_____

_____

_____

Write a rough draft of what the man smells.

_____

_____

_____

_____

_____

_____

_____

Rewrite your rough draft using your teacher's suggestions.

_____

_____

_____

_____

_____

_____

_____

Now put it all together. Write a finished copy of what the man sees, hears, and smells.

_____

_____

_____

HINT! If you are not proud of what you have written, take another look and make it better.

_____

_____

_____

_____

_____

_____

_____

_____

_____

_____

_____

_____

_____

_____

_____

_____

_____

_____

_____

_____

Write the final copy (revised and clean) of the two pieces: the perspectives of the mother and the groundskeeper.

Mother's perspective	**Groundskeeper's perspective**
_____	_____
_____	_____
_____	_____
_____	_____
_____	_____
_____	_____
_____	_____
_____	_____
_____	_____
_____	_____
_____	_____
_____	_____
_____	_____
_____	_____
_____	_____
_____	_____
_____	_____
_____	_____
_____	_____
_____	_____
_____	_____

Fill out the "Student Progress Report" on the next page.

Remember to fill out the writing skills mastery check-off form and, if necessary, to record spelling words and other problems that your need to address in the future.

CONTINUED ON NEXT PAGE➔

Student Progress Report

This is the best sentence I wrote this week:

_____

_____

_____

_____

I think it is the best because:

_____

_____

_____

_____

I made this mistake this week and this is what I learned to help me
avoid making the mistake again:

_____

_____

_____

_____

This is the sentence showing how I fixed the mistake:

_____

_____

_____

_____

Comments:

_____

_____

_____

_____

Your teacher will assign a book for you to read this week. Be sure to finish it before the end of the week. Review the five steps of reading literature and prepare to describe each of the five elements from your book.

Name of the book: _____

Author of the book: _____

Read and discuss with your teacher

This year, we have been studying different aspects of plot and its importance in studying literature. Plot is the storyline, but it is more than just the events that we read about. As readers, it is important that we understand the sequence of those events and how they relate to each other. It is also important that we understand how the characters affect the plot and how the plot affects them.

We also learned about different types of plot, including plot-driven stories and character-driven stories. We also learned about the different parts of a plot and practiced identifying those elements in a story. We also learned about the importance of conflict to a plot and the different types of conflict that exist in stories.

In the next two Reading Lessons, we're going to practice applying what we have learned while we finish up our studies of plots in literature.

Discussion Questions

Now that you have spent the year studying plots, what is your favorite plot in a story? Why is that one your favorite? Was that story your favorite plot before you studied plots this year? Do you think more about plots now when you are reading?

Objectives:

❶ Review key concepts about plot.

❷ Read the assigned Bible passage.

❸ Answer questions about the assigned Bible passage.

❹ Write a paragraph.

❺ Read and discuss an assigned book (teacher's choice).

Read and discuss assigned passage

Read the following Bible passage: Mark 15:1–39

Step One: Who is this passage about, and what is the cultural and historical setting?

_____

_____

_____

Step Two: What is the genre of this passage (history, poetry, prophecy, proverbs, letters, parables, etc.)?

_____

_____

_____

Step Three: What is the intended meaning of this passage? Some questions you can ask to help with this question are "What fallen or sinful condition is being highlighted in this passage?" or "What prompted the author to write this passage?" (Is this message about sin, salvation, faith, hope, etc.?)

_____

_____

_____

Step Four: Can you list other Bible passages that help define the intended meaning? (A concordance would be helpful here.)

_____

_____

_____

Step Five: Once the original meaning is understood, seek to find a simple life application.

_____

_____

_____

Read and discuss with your teacher

Answer the following questions about the passage:

1. What is the plot of this story (what are the events that happen)?

_____

_____

_____

2. Does the story have a recognizable beginning, middle, and end? How do you know?

_____

_____

_____

3. How does the plot connect with the story's theme? If you are not sure of what the story's theme is, think about the story's message. Does the plot connect to the message in some way?

_____

_____

_____

4. What is the exposition? What is the complication? What is the rising action? What is the climax? What is the falling action? What is the resolution?

_____

_____

_____

Complete the following activity

You will write a short, well-organized, 3-paragraph essay about plot in
this week's passage. You can choose to discuss any aspect of the plot.
You might want to talk about the connection between the plot and the
theme or how plot and character are connected. You may instead want
to look at cause and effect in the plot or write about the driving force
of the plot. You may also want to identify one of the elements of plot
(such as the complication or climax) and write about that. You may also
choose to examine conflict in the plot. Whatever you choose to do, just
pick one topic to write about.

HINT! In your
introduction, identify
what you are going to talk
about and your thoughts
on the subject. In the body
paragraph, explain your
reasons for drawing the
conclusions that you did
on the topic. Be sure to use
specific examples. Wrap
up your paper with a final
paragraph as a conclusion.

Read and discuss assigned book

Remember to keep in mind these five principles when reading the book of your choice this week:

Step One: Determine the genre of the literature (historical fiction, fantasy, drama, Western, mystery, science fiction, poetry, biography, etc.).

_____

_____

_____

Step Two: Read the book, keeping in mind the main setting of the text and the primary roles of each character.

_____

_____

_____

Step Three: Look for the flow of the story. Describe the flow of the story from your book.

_____

_____

_____

Step Four: What is the book's message or what do you think it is trying to teach you?

_____

_____

_____

CONTINUED ON NEXT PAGE→

Step Five: Does this message agree with what the Bible teaches? Why or why not?

_____

_____

_____

Prewriting

When you talk to your friends, all of the sentences you use are not of the same length. This is because you already understand how the length of your sentences can help your friends understand what you are saying. If you were telling your friend about a car crash, you would automatically change the lengths of your sentences. This example will convince you that you do this. You might structure your sentences this way:

> We were headed downtown. My brother and I heard this siren when we got to the corner at Main Street.

> We were on the sidewalk by the drug store and here comes this cop car. This old Buick is just starting out from the stop sign when he sees the flashing lights. He slams on the brakes. This guy behind him does not see him stop and bangs into him, hard. Crash! Boy, was that a mess, with glass all over.

This is the way people talk and that is the way good writers write dialogue. I tried to make this conversation sound real, and then I counted the words. This is what I found:

Paragraph I

Sentence 1. 4 words

2. 16 words

Paragraph II

Sentence 1. 15 words

2. 17 words

3. 5 words

4. 14 words

5. 1 word

6. 9 words

Today, listen to conversations and notice the varying lengths of sentences.

Objectives:

❶ Understand that sentence length is important.

❷ Control the length of your sentences to help your reader appreciate and understand what you have to say.

Writing

You will write about an event. It should be written in **third person** and **past tense**. Put dialogue in it that sounds like real people talking. This means that the sentences must be of different lengths.

An easy way to practice this is to create two people in conversation and have one of them be an adult and one of them be a child. You could write about a mother asking her son about cleaning his room. Or you could write about a young girl telling her mother what she wants for Christmas. (You will have to have the characters give fairly long speeches in order to give you an opportunity to vary the lengths of their sentences.)

HINT! Remember to put dialogue inside quotation marks, and the first letter is capitalized.

Example: Bill walked down the stairs and said to his mom, "I finished cleaning my room. Can I go outside now?"

_____

_____

_____

_____

_____

_____

_____

_____

_____

_____

_____

_____

_____

_____

_____

_____

_____

Ask your teacher to look at your work and suggest how to improve it.

Today you are to finish your writing. Review it for correct punctuation. Write a clean copy of it:

_____

_____

_____

_____

_____

_____

_____

_____

_____

_____

_____

_____

_____

_____

_____

_____

_____

_____

_____

_____

_____

Ask your teacher to look at your work and suggest how to improve it.

Writing
Lesson 18

Day
174

The Long and Short of It
Creative

Name

Write a final copy of your paper on the Creative Worksheet. This means that it will be neat and have no spelling or punctuation errors in it.

This is a short exercise, but it is an important one. You should practice using different length sentences even when you are describing things or writing letters to your friends. They will enjoy your letters more and so will you. Every time you write, think about sentence length variety.

Set your paper up this way:

```
                                              Your Name
                                              The Date

                      SPACE

                      SPACE

                   Your Title

                      SPACE


The Conversation


                      SPACE

                      SPACE

The sentence length analysis
```

CONTINUED ON NEXT PAGE ➔

Read your paper to a friend or family member. See if it sounds like a conversation and flows like a conversation a person would actually have.

Fill out the "Student Progress Report" on the next page.

Remember to fill out the writing skills mastery check-off form and, if necessary, to record spelling words and other problems that you need to address in the future.

Student Progress Report

This is the best sentence I wrote this week:

_____

_____

_____

_____

I think it is the best because:

_____

_____

_____

_____

I made this mistake this week and this is what I learned to help me avoid making the mistake again:

_____

_____

_____

_____

This is the sentence showing how I fixed the mistake:

_____

_____

_____

_____

Comments:

_____

_____

_____

_____

Your teacher will assign a book for you to read this week. Be sure to finish it before the end of the week. Review the five steps of reading literature and prepare to describe each of the five elements from your book.

Name of the book: _____

Author of the book: _____

Read and discuss with your teacher

We're going to finish reviewing plot this week. When you are reading, it is important to pay attention to the plot. Not only does it form the basis of the story, but it also gives us a deeper understanding of the characters and the themes.

A lot of times writers will follow the basic concepts that we learned about plots. For instance, they will provide exposition in the beginning, and they will write a clear resolution at the end. But that is not always the case. When you come across a story with an unusual plot, you need to stop and think about why the author is doing this. Is the author trying to tell you something? Is the author trying to get you to stop and think about this? Chances are, the answer is yes.

Discussion Questions

Think about all the Bible passages you have read this year for the class. Which one has your favorite plot? Why is it your favorite plot? Was it your favorite before studying plot this year? What's the most important/helpful thing you have learned about plots this year?

Objectives:

❶ Review key concepts about plot.

❷ Read the assigned Bible passage.

❸ Answer questions about the assigned Bible passage.

❹ Write a paragraph.

❺ Read and discuss an assigned book (teacher's choice).

Read and discuss assigned passage

Read the following Bible passage: Acts 27:1–28:2

Step One: Who is this passage about, and what is the cultural and historical setting?

_____

_____

_____

Step Two: What is the genre of this passage (history, poetry, prophecy, proverbs, letters, parables, etc.)?

_____

_____

_____

Step Three: What is the intended meaning of this passage? Some questions you can ask to help with this question are "What fallen or sinful condition is being highlighted in this passage?" or "What prompted the author to write this passage?" (Is this message about sin, salvation, faith, hope, etc.?)

_____

_____

_____

Step Four: Can you list other Bible passages that help define the intended meaning? (A concordance would be helpful here.)

_____

_____

_____

Step Five: Once the original meaning is understood, seek to find a simple life application.

_____

_____

_____

Read and discuss with your teacher

Answer the following questions about the passage:

1. What is the plot of this story (what are the events that happen)?

_____

_____

_____

2. Does the story have a recognizable beginning, middle, and end? How do you know?

_____

_____

_____

3. How does the plot connect with the story's theme? If you are not sure of what the story's theme is, think about the story's message. Does the plot connect to the message in some way?

_____

_____

_____

4. What is the exposition? What is the complication? What is the rising action? What is the climax? What is the falling action? What is the resolution?

_____

_____

_____

Complete the following activity

You will write a short, well-organized, 3-paragraph essay about plot in this week's passage. You can choose to discuss any aspect of the plot. You might want to talk about the connection between the plot and the theme or how plot and character are connected. You may instead want to look at cause and effect in the plot or write about the driving force of the plot. You may also want to identify one of the elements of plot (such as the complication or climax) and write about that. You may also choose to examine conflict in the plot. Whatever you choose to do, just pick one topic to write about.

HINT! In your introduction, identify what you are going to talk about and your thoughts on the subject. In the body paragraph, explain your reasons for drawing the conclusions that you did on the topic. Be sure to use specific examples. Wrap up your paper with a final paragraph as a conclusion.

_____

_____

_____

_____

_____

_____

_____

_____

_____

_____

_____

_____

_____

_____

_____

_____

_____

_____

_____

_____

_____

Read and discuss assigned book

Remember to keep in mind these five principles when reading the book of your choice this week:

Step One: Determine the genre of the literature (historical fiction, fantasy, drama, Western, mystery, science fiction, poetry, biography, etc.).

_____

_____

_____

Step Two: Read the book, keeping in mind the main setting of the text and the primary roles of each character.

_____

_____

_____

Step Three: Look for the flow of the story. Describe the flow of the story from your book.

_____

_____

_____

Step Four: What is the book's message or what do you think it is trying to teach you?

_____

_____

_____

Step Five: Does this message agree with what the Bible teaches? Why or why not?

_____

_____

_____

CONTINUED ON NEXT PAGE ➔

Problems I Have Solved This Second Semester

1. _____

_____

2. _____

_____

3. _____

_____

4. _____

_____

5. _____

_____

6. _____

_____

7. _____

_____

8. _____

_____

How I feel about this progress I am making:

_____

_____

“

My heart is overflowing with a good theme;

I recite my composition concerning the King;

My tongue is the pen of a ready writer.

Psalm 45:1

Helpful Terms

Ambiguity: An ambiguous statement may be taken in more than one way.

She saw the man walking down the street.

This can mean

    A. She saw the man as she was walking down the street.
    B. She saw the man who was walking down the street.

Often, a sentence is ambiguous because a pronoun (it, she, they, them) does not have a clear antecedent (what it refers to).

Bill looked at the coach when he got the money.

This can mean

    A. When Bill got the money, he looked at the coach.
    B. When the coach got the money, Bill looked at him.

Ambiguous statements should be rewritten so that the meaning is clear to the reader.

Apostrophe: An apostrophe (') is a mark used to indicate possession or contraction. Rules:

1. To form the possessive case (who owns it) of a singular noun (one person or thing), add an apostrophe and an *s*.

    Examples: *the girl's coat   James's ball   the car's tire*

2. To form the possessive case of a plural noun (two or more people or things) ending in *s*, add only the apostrophe.

    Examples: *the boys' car   the cars' headlights*

3. Do not use an apostrophe for *his, hers, its, ours, yours, theirs, whose*.

    Examples: *The car was theirs.   The school must teach its students.*

4. Indefinite pronouns (could be anyone), such as *one, everyone, everybody*, require an apostrophe and an *s* to show possession.

    Examples: *One's car is important.   That must be somebody's bat.*

5. An apostrophe shows where letters have been omitted in a contraction (making one word out of two). Note that the apostrophe goes in the word where the letter or letters have been left out.

   Examples: *can't* for *cannot*   *don't* for *do not*
   we've for *we have*   *doesn't* for *does not*

6. Use an apostrophe and an *s* to make the plural of letters, numbers, and of words referred to as words.

   Examples: *There are three b's and two m's in that sentence.*
   Do not say so many "and so's" when you explain things.

Audience: Writers do not just write. They write to specific readers in specific forms for specific purposes. To be effective, writers must decide what form is most appropriate for their intended readers so that they can accomplish their purposes.

Keep in mind that just as your students talk differently to different audiences, they must write differently also. They would not talk to you or their minister the same way they would talk to each other or their friends.

As you read your students' writing, think of who their intended audiences are and try to judge how what they are saying will influence those people.

1. Informal — colloquial (used with friends in friendly letters and notes):

Man, that was a such a dumb test. I just flunked it.

2. Semiformal (used in themes, tests, and term papers in school and in letters and articles to businesses and newspapers):

The test was very hard, so I did not do well.

3. Formal (seldom used by students but appropriate for the most formal of written communication on the highest levels of government, business, or education):

The six-week's examination was of sufficient scope to challenge the knowledge of the best of the students in the class. Not having adequately prepared for it, he did not demonstrate his true ability.

Awkward Writing: Awkward writing is rough and clumsy. It can be confusing to the reader and make the meaning unclear. Sometimes just the changing of the placement of a word or the changing of a word will clear up the awkwardness.

If you ask your students to read their work out loud or have someone else read it to them and listen to what is read, they can sometimes catch the awkwardness. Remember that they need to read loud enough to hear their own voices.

1. *Each of you will have to bring each day each of the following things: pen, pencil, and paper.*

   This should be rewritten to read:

Each day, bring pens, pencils, and paper.

2. *The bird flew down near the ground and, having done this, began looking for bugs or worms because it was easier to see them down low than it had been when it was flying high in the sky.*

There are many problems with that sentence. To get rid of its awkwardness, it could be rewritten to read:

   The bird, looking for food, swooped low.

Keep in mind that the point of your students' writing is for them to give their readers information. The simplest way to do this may be the best way.

Cliché: A cliché is a phrase or sentence that has become an overused stereotype. All children like to use expressions they have heard or read. It makes them feel that they are writing like adult authors. You will catch expressions that they do not realize have been used so many times before that they no longer are fresh and exciting for their readers:

pretty as a picture   *tall as a tree*   *snapped back to reality*

stopped in his tracks   *stone cold dead*   *flat on his face*

roared like a lion   *white as a sheet*   *graceful as a swan*

stiff as a board   *limber as a willow*

Usually the first expressions young writers think of when they write will be clichés. If you think you have heard an expression before, you might suggest they not use it, but help them think of new ways to tell the readers the same information.

Commas: Commas separate ideas and clarify meanings. Teachers often see comma usage as problematic, even though all writers have some comma placement rules they ignore. Keep in mind that children cannot learn all the comma rules at once, and some will never learn them all. To help your students with commas, teach them the basic patterns that require commas. They can then look for these sentence patterns in their own writing.

Rules: Your students should use commas in the following situations:

1. To separate place names — as in addresses, dates, or items in a series

2. To set off introductory or concluding expressions

3. To clarify the parts of a compound sentence

4. To set off transitional or non-restrictive words or expressions in a sentence

Examples:

1. *During the day on May 3, 1989, I began to study.*

   I had courses in English, math and geography at a little school in Ann Arbor, Michigan.

   The parts of the date should be separated by commas, and the courses in this sentence which come in a list should be separated by commas. Your students have a choice of whether to put a comma before the *and* just prior to the last item on a list.

2. *After the bad showing on the test, Bill felt he had to study more than he had.*

   A comma sets off the introduction — *After the bad showing on the test* — from the central idea of this sentence — *Bill felt he had to study more.*

3. *Bill went to class to study for the test, and I went to the snack bar to feed the inner beast.*

   There are two complete ideas here: 1) Bill went to study; and 2) I went to eat. These two ideas can be joined in a compound (two or more things put together) sentence with a comma and a conjunction (and, but, or) between them.

4. *Bob, who didn't really care, made only five points on the test.*

   Notice where the commas are placed in the example above. The idea of this fourth sentence is that Bob made only five points on the test. The information given that he did not care is interesting but not essential to understanding the main idea of the sentence. The commas indicate that the words between them are not essential to the meaning of the sentence.

Comma Splice: A comma splice is when the two halves of a compound sentence are joined/separated by a comma without an appropriate coordinating conjunction (and, or, but).

Example:

Bill had to take the test over again, he felt sorry he would miss the party.

This comma splice can be avoided by writing this sentence in one of the four following ways:

1. *Bill had to take the test over again and felt sorry he would miss the party.*

2. *Bill had to take the test over again, and he felt sorry he would miss the party.*

3. *Bill had to take the test over again; he felt sorry he would miss the party.*

4. *Bill had to take the test over again. He felt sorry he would miss the party.*

Notice that the punctuation in each of the above examples shows a different relationship between the two ideas. For example, correcting a comma splice by adding a coordinating conjunction and a comma indicates that two ideas are connected much more than separating them with a period does. Using a semicolon to correct a comma splice indicates more of a connection between the ideas than a period would but less of a connection than a comma and coordinating conjunction does.

Dialogue Structure and Punctuation: Dialogue is conversation between two or more people. When shown in writing, it refers to the speech or thoughts of characters.

Rule: Dialogue can occur either in the body of the writing or on a separate line for each new speaker.

Note: When writing by hand, use quotation marks for both external and internal dialogue. It is appropriate to use italics for internal dialogue when typing.

Examples:

1. John took his test paper from the teacher and said to him, "This looks like we'll get to know each other well." The teacher looked surprised and said with a smile, "I hope so."

2. John took his test paper from the teacher and said to him, "This looks like you and I'll get to know each other well."

   The teacher looked surprised and said with a smile, "I hope so."

3. John took his test paper from the teacher and thought, *This looks like I'll get to know this old man well this year.* The teacher looked surprised — as if he had read John's mind — and thought, *I hope so.*

Diction: Diction is the specific selection of words. There are at least four levels of diction:

1. Formal: The words of educated people when they are being serious with each other

Example: *Our most recent suggestion was the compromise we felt we could make under the present circumstances.*

2. Informal: Polite conversation of people who are relaxed

   Example: *We have given you the best offer we could.*

3. Colloquial: Everyday speech by average people

   Example: *That was the best we could do.*

4. Slang: Ways of talking that are never used in writing except to show characterization in dialogue

   Example: *It's up to you, cook or get outta the kitchen.*

Flowery Writing: Your students will use flowery writing when they want to impress their readers (you) with how many good words they can use to express ideas. This results in the words used becoming more important than the ideas presented.

Rule: A general rule that should apply is: What your students say should be put as simply as possible.

Example:

The red and fiery sun slowly settled into the distant hills like some great, billowing sailing ship sinking beyond the horizon. It cast its pink and violet flags along the tops of the clouds where they waved briefly before this ship of light slid beneath the waves of darkness and cast us all, there on the beach, into night.

This is so flowery that it is hard to read without laughing. It should be rewritten to read:

We remained on the beach gazing at the darkening sky while the sun set.

Fragment: This is part of a sentence which lacks a subject or a verb or both. Check your students' sentences to make sure they have both subjects and verbs. They should avoid using fragments in their expository papers.

Some writers use fragments effectively. Your students may do this in their creative writing. Fragments can be powerful if used correctly:

When Janet reached her door she found it was partly open. A burglar! Someone had been in her house and had left the door open.

In this example. "A burglar!" is an effective fragment because it helps emphasize Janet's surprise. Unless a student is trying to achieve a specific effect in creative writing, fragments should be avoided.

Modifier (Dangling): A modifier should be placed as close as possible to what it is modifying so that there is no ambiguity. A dangling modifier is a modifier that is not placed next to what it modifies, which is confusing for the reader.

Examples:

1. *Getting up, my arms felt tired.* (How did the arms get up all by themselves?) This should read: *When I got up, my arms felt tired.*

2. *Coming down the street, my feet wanted to turn into the park.* (Again, how did the feet do this?) This should read: *Coming down the street, I felt as if my feet wanted to turn toward the park.*

3. *Being almost asleep, the accident made me jump.* (It is clear the accident could not have been asleep.) This should read: *I was almost asleep, and the accident made me jump.*

Omitted Words: Children often leave words out of sentences, or they leave the endings off from words. You can help them with this problem if you have them read their work out loud and slowly. Insist that they read slowly so that you can catch every syllable. Depending on the reasons behind the omissions, reading aloud can help your students catch the words they have left out.

Paragraph: A paragraph is a sentence or a group of sentences developing one idea or topic. In nonfiction writing, a paragraph consists of a topic sentence and other sentences that support the topic sentence with additional details. A good guideline is that a paragraph in expository writing should have at least four supportive sentences, making at least five sentences for every paragraph.

A topic sentence is one sentence that introduces the reader to the main idea of the paragraph. Paragraph development may be made by facts, examples, incidents, comparison, contrast, definition, reasons (in the form of arguments), or by a combination of methods.

Parallelism: Two or more parts of a sentence or list that have equal importance should be structured in the same way. In a list, the items must be the same part of speech.

Examples:

1. *We went home to eat and reading.*

This should read: *We went home to eat and to read.* This is obvious in such a short sentence, but this is an easy mistake to make when the sentence is complicated.

2. *There are a number of things that a boy must think about when he is planning to take a bike trip. He must think about checking the air pressure in his tires, putting oil on the chain, making sure the batteries in his light are fresh, and to make sure his brakes work properly.*

   Notice that in this list there is a combination of three parallel participles and one infinitive, which is not parallel in structure. (This sounds like English-teacher talk.) What it means is the first three items on the list (*checking*, *putting*, and *making*) are parallel, but the fourth item on the list (*to make*) is not parallel because it is not structured the same way.

This sentence should be rewritten to read: *He must think about checking the air pressure in his tires, putting oil on the chain, making sure the batteries in his light are fresh, and making sure his brakes work properly.*

Pronoun Reference and Agreement: To keep writing from being boring, pronouns are often used instead of nouns.

Rule: It must be clear to the reader which noun the pronoun is replacing. The pronoun must agree in case, gender, and number with that noun. The most common error young writers make is with number agreement.

Examples:

1. *Betty and Janet went to the show, but she didn't think it was so good.* (It is not clear which girl did not like the show.)

2. *If a child comes to dinner without clean hands, they must go back to the sink and wash over.* (The word *they* refers to a child, and the number is mixed. This should read: *If children come to dinner without clean hands, they should go back. . . .*)

3. *Both boys took exams, but Bob got a higher score on it.* (The pronoun *it* refers to the noun *exams*. The number is mixed here.)

4. *Everybody should go to the show, and they should have their tickets handy.* (The problem here is that the word *everybody* is singular, but the pronouns *they* and *their* are plural.) The following words are singular and they need singular verbs: *everybody, anybody, each, someone.*

Quotation Marks: Quotation marks are used to indicate exact words and to indicate the titles of short works and chapters of long works.

Rules:

1. Your students should put quotation marks around direct quotations (someone's exact words).

When they use other marks of punctuation with quotation marks, they should put commas and periods inside the quotation marks.

Other punctuation marks (e.g., question mark, exclamation mark) go inside the quotation marks if they are part of the quotation; if they are not part of the quotation, they go outside the quotation marks.

Example: *The salesman said, "This is the gum all the kids are chewing."*

Example: *Is that why he said, "Come here right now"?*

2. Put quotation marks around the titles of chapters, articles, other parts of books or magazines, short poems, short stories and songs.

Example: *In this magazine there were two things I really liked: "The Wind Blows Free" and "Flowers," the poems by the young girl.*

Redundancy: Redundancy means using different words to say the same thing. The writer does not gain by this, it only confuses and bores the reader.

Examples: *I, myself, feel it is true.*   *It is plain and clear to see.*

In the first sentence, "I" and "myself" means the same thing. The sentence can just be "I feel it is true."

In the second sentence, "plain" and "clear" mean the same thing, so only one of them is needed: "It is plain to see." "It is clear to see."

This is an easy mistake to make, and it will take conscious thought for your students to avoid this problem. You will have to help them find redundancies in their work. There are no exercises they can do that will help. Just have them use care when they are proofreading their work.

Run-On Sentence: This is the combining of two or more sentences as if they were one without appropriate punctuation. Run-on sentences should be fixed by breaking them into multiple sentences or by adding appropriate punctuation (see "Commas").

Example:

Bill saw that the fish was too small he put it back in the lake and then put a fresh worm on his hook.

Any of the ways to fix a comma splice can also fix a run-on sentence. This sentence could be broken into two sentences by putting a period or a semicolon between *small* and *he*. It could also be rewritten to read:

Bill saw that the fish was too small, so he put it back in the lake and put a fresh worm on his hook.

Sentence Variety: Young writers have a tendency to structure all or most of their sentences in the same way. You need to help your students give variety to the structuring of their sentences. A common problem for young writers is that of beginning most sentences with a subject-verb pattern.

Example:

Janet bought a car. The car was blue. It had a good radio. She liked her car and spent a lot of time in it.

These sentences could be re-written and combined so that they all do not start with a subject and verb.

The car Janet bought was blue. Because she liked it so much, she spent a lot of time in it.

Subject-Verb Agreement (Number): Closely related words have matching forms, and when the forms match, they agree. Subjects and their verbs agree if they both are singular or both are plural.

Rules: Singular subjects require singular verbs, and plural subjects require plural verbs.

Singular: *car man   that   she*

Plural: *cars men   those   they*

Singular: *The heater was good.   The heater works well.*

Plural: *The heaters were good.   The heaters work well.*

Most nouns form their plural by adding the letter *s*, as in *bats* and *cats*. The clue is the final *s*. It is just the opposite with most verbs. A verb ending in *s* is usually singular, as in *puts, yells, is,* and *was.*

Most verbs not ending in *s* are plural, as in *they put, they yell.* The exceptions are verbs used with *I* and singular *you: I put, you put.*

Most problems come when there is a phrase or clause between the subject and the verb. Example:

This red car, which is just one of a whole lot full of cars, is owned by John and Bob.

(It is easy for some young writers to think that *cars* is the plural subject and write the sentence this way: *This red car, which is just one of a whole lot full of cars, are owned by John and Bob.* The subject of this sentence (*This red car*) is singular; there are just a lot of words between the subject and the verb, and it confuses the number.)

Tense Error: Tense errors occur when past and present tenses are mixed without justification. Rules:

1. Present tense is used to describe actions that are taking place at the time of the telling of the event.

    Example: *John is in the house. Mr. Jones lives there.*

2. Past tense is used to describe actions that have already happened.

    Example: *John was in the house. Mr. Jones lived there.*

3. Future tense is used to describe actions that will happen.

    Example: *John will be in the house. Mr. Jones will live there.*

Transitions: Transitions are bridges from one idea to the next or from one reference to the next or from one section of a paper to the next.

Rule: Writers should use transitions to bridge ideas for their readers by

1. using linking words (*however, moreover, thus,* and *because*) and phrases like *on the other hand, in effect,* and *as an example.*

2. repeating words and phrases used earlier in the writing.

3. referring to points used previously. Examples:

If your student writes two paragraphs about pets, one about a cat and one about a dog, your student should transition between the two paragraphs. Below, the idea of having fun with the cat will help transition to the paragraph about having fun with the dog. *On the other hand* is a transition phrase that helps the reader move between the two ideas.

> *. . .and so I have a lot of fun with my cat.*

> *My dog, on the other hand, is fun for different reasons. We spend time. . .*

Unconscious Repetition:
Unconscious repetition will distract the reader, create unnecessarily wordy language, or emphasize parts of a passage that do not need to be emphasized. Conscious repetition is fine so long as it serves a deliberate purpose.

> *To select magazines which are written on the reader's level of reading and interest, a person should select magazines that reflect his economic and intellectual level.*

This could be re-written to read:

> *A person should select magazines to fit his reading ability, interest, and budget.*

Unconscious Rhyming:
Unconscious rhyming happens when a writer accidentally uses words that rhyme. The rhyming words will ring in the reader's mind and detract from what the writer wants the reader to think about.

> *The man was feeling really well until he fell.*

The sentence could be re-written to read:

> *The man was feeling really well until he stumbled on the driveway and slid under the greasy truck.*

Voice (Passive and Active):
Most sentences are built on the order of subject-verb-object. This produces an active voice. If a passive verb is used, it inverts this order and makes it seem as if the object were doing rather than receiving the action of the verb.

Your students' writing will be more forceful if they use active voice.

Examples:

Active:	Bill threw the ball.	We must spend this money.
Passive:	The ball was thrown by Bill.	This money must be spent by us.

Your students can use a passive voice if:

1. The doer of the action is unknown

2. The action needs to be emphasized

3. The receiver of the action is of more importance than the doer of the action.

Examples:

1. *When we were gone, the house was burglarized.* (The person who broke in is unknown.)

2. *No matter how hard they played, the game was lost.* (The game being lost is the most important thing.)

3. *My pet mouse was eaten by that cat.* (The mouse is more important than the cat.)

Wrong Word: The words your students use do not always mean what they think they do.

Rule: Your students should not use words in their writing that they do not use when speaking. If they would never say the words *alas* or *to no avail* or *travail,* they should not write them.

Reading Lesson #1 – Day 7

1. The serpent tempts Eve; Adam and Eve eat the forbidden fruit; Adam and Eve hide from God; God curses the serpent, Eve, and Adam; God drives Adam and Eve from the Garden of Eden.

2. Yes. In the beginning, Adam and Eve live in the Garden of Eden. In the middle, they disobey God's commands. In the end, they are forced to leave the Garden of Eden.

3. The story's theme is about the Fall of man and how sin entered the world through human disobedience. The story's plot shows this happening when Adam and Eve eat the fruit and suffer the consequences for their actions.

Reading Lesson #2 – Day 17

1. God tested Abraham by commanding him to sacrifice his son Isaac; Abraham was obedient and was prepared to sacrifice his son; God stopped him and provided a ram in Isaac's place; God blessed Abraham for his obedience.

2. Yes. In the beginning, God decides to test Abraham by ordering him to sacrifice Isaac. In the middle, Abraham prepares to follow through with this command. In the end, God stops Abraham and blesses him.

3. The theme is about obedience to God. The story tells us about how God tested Abraham and then blessed him for his obedience.

Day 19

10, 2, 5, 1, 6, 8, 11, 4, 7, 9, 3

Reading Lesson #3 – Day 27

1. Esau and Jacob are twins but are very different from each other; Esau sells his birthright to Jacob; Isaac is going to bless Esau and asks him to go hunting; Rebecca and Jacob trick Isaac into blessing Jacob instead.

2. Yes. In the beginning, Esau sells his birthright to Jacob. In the middle, Isaac decides to bless Esau. In the end, Isaac is tricked into blessing Jacob instead.

3. The story's theme is one of family conflict, which is illustrated by the story of the two brothers.

Reading Lesson #4 – Day 37

1. Joseph is Jacob's favorite son; Jacob's other sons are jealous of Joseph; Joseph has a dream about reigning over his brothers; Joseph's brothers conspired to kill him; Reuben tried to save him by throwing him in a pit; Judah suggests selling him to some Midianite traders; Joseph's brothers sell him into slavery and he is taken to Egypt; Joseph's brothers pretend that he has been killed.

2. Yes. In the beginning, Joseph is Jacob's favorite and his brothers are jealous. In the middle, the other brothers conspire to kill Joseph. In the end, he is sold into slavery and they pretend he is dead.

3. The theme is one of family conflict and is illustrated by the story of Joseph and his brothers' jealousy of him.

Reading Lesson #5 – Day 47

1. God appears to Moses in the burning bush; God tells Moses that He is sending him to lead the Hebrews out of Egypt; Moses is hesitant; God gets irritated with Moses and tells him to use his brother Aaron as a spokesman; Moses leaves for Egypt.

2. Yes. In the beginning, Moses is tending his father-in-law's flocks and God speaks to him. In the middle, Moses keeps offering excuses for why he cannot be the one to lead the Hebrews out of Egypt. In the end, God has countered all of Moses' excuses, and he leaves for Egypt.

3. The theme of this story is of being called by God. We see this through the story of Moses' resistance and God's insistence.

Reading Lesson #6 – Day 57

1. The Midianites are oppressing the Israelites; an angel appears to Gideon; the angel tells Gideon

that he will defeat the Midianites; Gideon tests the angel; Gideon tears down his father's pagan altar.

2. Yes. In the beginning, Gideon is threshing wheat. In the middle, the angel calls Gideon. In the end, Gideon tears down his father's altar.

3. The theme is about trusting the Lord. In the story, Gideon is initially afraid and reluctant, but he eventually accepts God's call.

Day 59

The exposition is the opening verses that explain how Midian has conquered the Israelites and the harsh way the Midianites treat them: Judges 6:1–10. It provides necessary context to help readers understand why Gideon was called and also why he may have been reluctant to respond.

Reading Lesson #7 – Day 67

1. An Israelite family moves to Moab to escape a famine. The men in the family die, leaving the Israelite woman and her Moabite daughters-in-law to fend for themselves. Naomi, the mother-in-law, tells the other two women to go back to Moab. Ruth insists on staying with her, so they travel together to Israel.

2. Yes. In the beginning, Naomi moves to Moab with her husband and sons. In the middle, the husband and sons have died and she decides to return to Israel. In the end, Ruth decides to go with her and they travel to Israel.

3. The theme of the story is loyalty. Ruth demonstrates loyalty in her refusal to leave Naomi.

Day 69

The complication is when the men in her family die, leaving her and her daughters-in-law on their own. Some might argue the complication is when Naomi decides to leave, but the death of her husband and sons are the cause of this decision, so that event is the complication.

Reading Lesson #8 – Day 77

1. God has rejected King Saul. God tells Samuel that He has chosen the next king from Jesse's sons. Samuel goes to Jesse's house and God has not chosen any of the sons that are there.

Finally, Samuel asks if Jesse has any more sons, and he sends for David, the youngest. Samuel anoints him. Samuel leaves.

2. Yes. In the beginning, God is unhappy with Saul and has chosen another to be king. In the middle, Samuel is at Jesse's house to find and anoint the next king. In the end, David is anointed.

3. The theme of the story is God's rejection of Saul and His calling of David. The story illustrates this by showing how David was anointed.

Day 79

God tells Samuel to anoint a new king from one of the sons of Jesse. The rising action occurs as Saul meets each of Jesse's older sons one by one in order to discover who the Lord has chosen to be king. Using human wisdom, Samuel would have chosen one of these sons to anoint, but the Lord instructs him that He does not judge as a man judges but instead looks at the heart of a man. This series of events leads to the climax when the Lord tells him to anoint David, the youngest and least likely to be king.

Reading Lesson #9 – Day 87

1. Esther needs to go to the king to protect her fellow Jews. She could be killed for going to him without being summoned. She and the others pray and fast. She goes to the king. He is happy to see her. She invites him and Haman to a banquet. Haman is jealous of her relative Mordechai and builds a gallows for him. At the banquet, Esther pleads with the king. The king is angry and has Haman killed.

2. Yes. In the beginning, Haman is plotting to kill all the Jews. In the middle, Mordechai asks Esther to intercede with the king. In the end, she does, and Haman is killed.

3. The theme of the story is how God works His will through people. Esther's story illustrates this through her courage in using her position to protect her people.

Day 89

The plot climax is the banquet scene when Haman's scheme is revealed to the king.

Reading Lesson #10 – Day 97

1. Nehemiah gets sad news about the state of Jerusalem. Nehemiah is upset by the news. He works for the king, who asks him what is wrong. Nehemiah tells him and asks for permission to go to Jerusalem to rebuild the city. The king agrees and helps Nehemiah make arrangements. Nehemiah travels to Jerusalem and looks at the destruction.

2. Yes. In the beginning, Nehemiah is upset by the news from Jerusalem. In the middle, he asks permission to rebuild the city. In the end, he travels there to start rebuilding.

3. The theme of the story is God-fearing leadership. Nehemiah's story demonstrates this in its depiction of his desire to rebuild the city.

4. There really is not exposition here. It is part of the complication, which is when Nehemiah learns that the city is in ruin. The rising action is Nehemiah's prayer and his unhappiness in front of the king. The climax is when he asks for permission to rebuild the city.

Day 99

The falling action is the king giving Nehemiah permission and the following arrangements for him to conduct the work.

Reading Lesson #11 – Day 107

1. Jonah preaches in Nineveh and tells the people they will be punished if they do not repent. The people of Nineveh repent, and God has mercy on them. Jonah is angry and goes outside the city to see what happens. God grows a plant to give him shade and then brings a worm to kill it. Jonah is angry about the death of the plant and the heat. God chastises Jonah for his mean attitude.

2. Yes. In the beginning, Jonah calls for the people of the city to repent. In the middle, the people repent, and Jonah becomes angry. In the end, God chastises Jonah.

3. The theme of the story is God's mercy and His desire for all to be saved. That theme is illustrated in the story of Nineveh repenting and the way God deals with Jonah's anger over that mercy.

4. There is not separate exposition here. That is combined with the complication, which is when God tells Jonah to go to Nineveh and preach to the city. The rising action is when Jonah arrives at the city and preaches and the city repents. The climax is God deciding to spare the city. The falling action is Jonah's anger over God's mercy.

Day 109

The resolution is at the end when God tells Jonah that he has no right to be angry at God for being merciful to people who have repented and that he has no right to be angry about the death of the plant.

Reading Lesson #12 – Day 117

1. Lazarus is sick. The disciples do not understand that Lazarus is dead, though Jesus knows. Jesus arrives and visits with Lazarus' sisters. Jesus raises Lazarus from the dead.

2. Yes. In the beginning, Lazarus is sick, and Jesus knows he will die. In the middle, Jesus arrives after Lazarus has died. In the end, Jesus raises Lazarus from the dead.

3. The theme of this story is faith. The story shows the different characters' faith through their reaction to Lazarus' death.

4. The exposition tells the reader who Lazarus is and who his sisters are. The complication is also given in the exposition — Lazarus is sick. The rising action includes Jesus and the disciples talking about Lazarus being sick and Jesus traveling to Lazarus' home and being told Lazarus is dead. The climax is when Jesus goes to Lazarus' tomb. The falling action is the discussion between Jesus and Mary. The resolution is Jesus raising Lazarus from the dead.

Reading Lesson #13 – Day 127

1. Jesus is teaching in the synagogues. He returns to His hometown of Nazareth and teaches in the synagogue. The people of Nazareth are hostile toward Him. He is driven out of the town.

2. Yes. In the beginning, Jesus is teaching in the synagogues. In the middle, He returns to His hometown of Nazareth and teaches. In the end, He is driven out.

3. The theme is one of rejection, and it is illustrated through how Jesus is treated.

4. The exposition is the opening verses that mention Jesus has started His ministries and is preaching throughout Galilee. The complication is His return to His hometown. The rising action is the response of the people. The climax is when the people become angry and try to throw Him over a cliff. The falling action is Him getting away, which is tied to the resolution of Him leaving Nazareth.

Reading Lesson #14 – Day 137

1. Jesus heals a blind man. The Pharisees question him and his parents about his healing. The Pharisees become mad at the healed man and cast him out. Jesus finds him, and He learns that the man believes in Him.

2. Yes. In the beginning, Jesus heals a blind man. In the middle, the man who was healed gets in trouble with the Pharisees. In the end, the man who was healed is found by Jesus, and the man believes in Him.

3. The theme is faith, and it is illustrated by the healed man's faith in Jesus at the end of the story.

4. The exposition is the initial conversation Jesus has with His disciples on what causes blindness. The complication is Jesus healing the blind man. The rising action is when the Pharisees question this man and his parents. The climax is when the Pharisees cast the healed man out. The falling action is Jesus finding him again. The resolution is the man believing in Jesus.

Reading Lesson #15 – Day 147

1. A crowd of people, including Pharisees, have gathered around Jesus. A man who is paralyzed is taken there by his friends, but they cannot get through. They lower the man into the room Jesus is in. The Pharisees are hostile, and Jesus heals him.

2. Yes. In the beginning, Jesus is in a crowd, and the paralyzed man's friends cannot reach Jesus. In the middle, they lower their friend through the roof for him to be healed. In the end, he is healed.

3. The theme of the story is faith. This is demonstrated through the contrast between

the faith of the paralyzed man's friends and the Pharisees' lack of faith.

4. The exposition is in the first verse, which explains the setting and situation. The complication is when the friends of the paralyzed man come but cannot get through the crowd. The rising action is the friends of the man lowering him into the room. The climax is when the Pharisees challenge Jesus. The falling action is Jesus responding to them, with the resolution being Him healing the man.

Day 149

The conflict between the paralyzed man's friends and the setting would be them struggling with the crowd/the building before going on top of the roof.

Reading Lesson #16 – Day 157

1. Jesus goes to the garden to pray. Judas betrays Jesus. Jesus is arrested. Peter follows along but denies Jesus three times.

2. Yes. In the beginning, Jesus is praying in the garden because He knows what will happen soon. In the middle, He is arrested. In the end, Peter denies Jesus.

3. The theme is willingness. This theme is developed through contrasting Jesus' behavior with Peter's.

4. The exposition is in the very first verse, where it notes the setting. The complication can be several moments, both of which happen before this story takes place. On one hand, Judas deciding to betray Jesus is one of the complications. On the other hand, Jesus already seems to be upset before the story starts, which is why He is in prayer. One could also argue that the complication is that God had always intended for these events to happen. The rising action is the prayer and the disciples sleeping. The climax is the arrest, with the falling action being Peter following and denying Jesus. The resolution is Peter weeping after he realized what he has done. This story might seem harder to break down by plot elements, and that is partially because it involves internal conflict.

Reading Lesson #17 – Day 167

1. Jesus is taken to Pilate, and He is questioned. Pilate offers the crowd a choice between Barabbas and Jesus. The crowd wants Jesus crucified. Pilate releases Barabbas and gives them Jesus after He is whipped. Jesus is mocked and taken away to be crucified. Jesus is crucified. Jesus dies.

2. Yes. In the beginning, Jesus is delivered to Pilate. In the middle, Jesus is taken to be crucified. In the end, He dies on the Cross.

3. The theme is sacrifice, which is illustrated by Jesus' suffering and dying on the Cross.

4. The exposition is very brief at the beginning in saying what happens before Jesus is handed over to Pilate. The complication is Jesus being handed over to Pilate, though one could also argue the complication occurred earlier. The rising action is Pilate offering the crowd Jesus or Barabbas and the crowd wanting Jesus crucified, as well as the punishment and mockery Jesus endures. The climax is Jesus being crucified. In the falling action, people continue to mock him, and the soldiers cast lots for His clothing. The resolution is His death, which causes the temple veil to tear and the centurion to recognize that He was the Son of God.

Reading Lesson #18 – Day 177

1. Paul is a prisoner and is sailing to Rome. The ship stops at several cities. Paul tries to warn the sailors that the journey will be dangerous, but he is ignored. They sail into a bad storm that lasts for days. Throughout, Paul tries to offer helpful advice. The ship is run aground, but Paul and the other prisoners are saved by the centurion onboard. The ship ran aground in Malta, and the locals are kind to the shipwreck survivors.

2. Yes. In the beginning, Paul is at the start of his journey to Rome. In the middle, he and his ship are caught in a terrible storm. In the end, he and the ship are shipwrecked in Malta.

3. The story's theme is having faith in God, which Paul demonstrates by his actions throughout the story.

4. The exposition is the information about the early sailing in the journey. The complication is that sailing is now dangerous. The rising action involves the storms and the difficulties at sea. The climax is when the ship runs aground. The falling action is the centurion rescuing Paul. The resolution is everyone on the ship making it safely to shore and being treated kindly by the local people.